a Consumer Publication

GETTING A NEW JOB

Consumers' Association
publishers of **Which?**
14 Buckingham Street
London WC2N 6DS

CONTENTS

Leaving a job	*page* 7
Between jobs	10
Applying for jobs	19
Interviews	41
Being offered a job	54
Pension scheme	54
Accepting a job	67
Being an employee	73
Contract of employment	74
Pay and hours	78
In the job	92
Discrimination	94
Maternity	98
Illness and accidents	101
Discipline	110
Dismissal	115
Industrial tribunal	125
Redundancy	132
Being unemployed	149
Index	164

Leaving a job

If you are in a job, there have to be very strong reasons for leaving. Any such change entails risk and stress, so review stringently your reasons for wanting to change jobs.

You may find yourself in a mood to give in your notice for various reasons

- principle – really? often 'principle' is no more than pride about losing an argument
- frustration – OK, but what about the frustration of no job?
- 'flash' row – never let the word 'resign' pass your lips (not worth it just for self-righteous satisfaction)
- personality clash – but how about your next job if you are so prickly?
- career prospects not there – have you asked? or is grass merely seeming greener elsewhere?
- another job to go to.

In the present economic and employment conditions, it would be foolish voluntarily to leave one job without having another to go to. And even if you have one lined up, unless you know a lot about the organisation you are going to join, there is a risk that the new job will not turn out to be the elysium that – from the outside – you think it will be.

giving notice

If you decide to resign of your own accord, you should plan matters carefully. The initiative is with you entirely. You may be able to come to arrangements which are flexible and suit both you and your employer.

First, you need to check how much notice your contract of employment requires you to give your employer. How is the period to be reckoned – from the date you give notice? or from the end of the calendar month in which you give notice? or is there some other arrangement? You should be able to get this information from the original letter of appointment or contract or statement you had from your employer, or from the employee handbook or staff notes. If there is nothing specified, by law you need give only one week's notice.

Try to gauge, in the light of what has happened when other staff resigned, what your employer's response will be. Will you be obliged to work your full notice period? or is your employer likely to ask you to leave at once, with or without pay for the unworked notice period?

If a salary change is close (for example, a cost of living increase, an annual increment, an anniversary review or a merit review), you may do better to delay your resignation until the change has been implemented, so that you have a higher salary base from which to negotiate with your next employer. If a bonus payment is due or a qualifying period is almost finished, it may be to your advantage to delay your resignation.

A very important factor is what will happen to your (eventual) pension from your employer's pension scheme. Interruption can have a significant effect. You are likely to find that you would be worse off as a result of changing jobs.

effect on pension

Changing your job, even from one company with a good pension scheme to another company with a good pension scheme, can result in a drastic reduction in your pension entitlement. A simple but realistic example shows what an effect this can have.

Mr Stay and Mr Move both belong to the pension scheme of their employer Company A. This fairly typical scheme provides a pension at the age of 65 of 1/60th of final salary for each year of service. After 20 years with the company, both men, now aged 45, are earning £9000 per annum. Mr Move changes his job and gets £9000 per annum from Company B, which has an identical pension scheme to Company A. He remains entitled to a pension at the age of 65 from Company A; this deferred pension will be 20/60ths × 9000 = £3000 a year.

For the next 20 years, inflation runs at about 10 per cent per annum, and both men's salaries increase more or less in line with inflation. By retirement at 65, both are earning £72,000 a year. Mr Move receives a pension from Company B of 20/60ths × 72,000 = £24,000 a year which, together with his pension of £3000 from Company A, gives him a total pension from the two companies of £27,000 a year. Mr Stay, on the other hand, gets 40/60ths × 72,000 = £48,000 a year.

In careers with identical salaries and identical pension schemes, Mr Stay gets a pension of, in round figures, 67 per cent of his final salary, Mr Move ends up with a pension of around 37 per cent of his final salary.

Thus, if you change jobs even once in mid-career, you are likely to be at a disadvantage from a pension point of view. The greater the number of changes, the greater the disadvantage is likely to be. If Mr Move were to change jobs at the ages of 35 and 45 and 55, with his salary at £3000 and £9000 and £27,000 respectively, his pension would be £500 + £1500 + £4500 + £12,000 = £18,500 a year – only 26 per cent of his final salary of £72,000.

This disadvantage of changing jobs normally applies irrespective of whether you keep your pension frozen in the scheme you leave or transfer its value to the scheme of your new employer.

On the other hand, there may be circumstances in which you would be wise to change your job in order to get into a good pension scheme. If you are not in a pension scheme at all or are in a poor one, or in any case plan to leave in due course, it could be to your advantage from a pension point of view to move soon.

The report on what to look for when changing your job in *Money Which*? September 1981 includes points about pensions.

negotiating better pension terms

Pension schemes should be designed for movers as well as for stayers. Employers who want to encourage staff mobility should realise that if they have a pension scheme offering the typical deferred pension, they are discouraging people, particularly in the 40 and 50 age groups, from changing jobs.

The time for employees to negotiate for better terms for leavers is while they are working for the employer whose scheme it is, and contributing to its funds. Deferred pensioners' interests are unlikely to be near the top of the list of priorities of those who decide on improvements to the pension scheme, and deferred pensioners are not around to defend their own interests.

You can always try to negotiate when you are leaving, but if you are leaving because you want to, you do not have much leverage.

between jobs

When, for whatever reason, you have finished with one job, and are going to set about landing the next one, use the break positively and take the opportunity to look objectively at your experience, your aspirations and the reality of your future. You probably have not had the chance to do so since you first began working 'n' years ago. Now you have the opportunity and the benefit of your experience to draw on to decide what sort of job you can do, want to do, can afford to do, next. Perhaps there are other jobs which can be done even more successfully and with greater enjoyment than the last one. You may have done the last job because it was there, but you may be capable of doing an entirely different job with much greater rewards.

taking stock

First of all, take stock. Write down the saleable attributes you can offer a prospective employer

- education
- work experience
- the industries, markets, fields you know something about
- other experience
- training you have received, both work-related and other
- other strengths, such as foreign languages
- interests, hobbies (these may have some job potential).

Next, based on this information and your self-knowledge, write down objectively

- what, overall, you think your strengths are
- what you have been competent at/happy doing
- what your weaknesses are
- what gaps you have in your experience
- what tasks/types of work you have felt uncomfortable/not good at.

Say to yourself 'If I could start again, I would . . .' and the answer should reveal

- preferred type of job
- preferred type of employer (or self-employment)
- preferred location.

An objective friend can be a great help in drawing out from you your strengths and weaknesses – you might easily be unrealistic in your own assessment, or underrate a valuable asset.

When you have thought through your aims and the attributes you could offer a potential employer, try your ideas out on people who will give you honest reactions.

If you have left your employment on good terms, go and see your former boss: she or he is someone who should be able to give you useful feedback on your strong and weak points – be prepared to hear between the lines. Former colleagues may have views about your shortcomings (if you can listen without bristling) and possibly about your strengths.

professional counselling

You may perhaps want to consider getting more professional counselling. If you are prepared to pay a fee (or your former employer can be persuaded to sponsor you), there are many commercial organisations who offer assessment and career counselling. Fees are high, so find out what the fee covers before committing yourself. Different organisations offer different types of services: counselling, vocational guidance, self-marketing, job-finding – and sometimes these overlap.

Occupational or vocational guidance is purely advisory and does not set out to help people find jobs.

Normally, you are given a number of tests and an interview. The tests include questions to find out about your

interests – arts/social/research/outdoor
personality – leadership/self-sufficiency/extroversion/confidence/sociability/conformity
aptitude – decision-making/teaching/administering/figure work/mechanical/writing/creativeness/manual/speaking.

The results of these tests are then compared with the profile of people doing various jobs. The idea is that if your profile is seen to match that of other people happily doing certain types of job, such a job will suit you, too.

At the interview, the career consultant will explain the test results, relate them to you as an individual and to your qualifications, and suggest a number of possible career paths.

A report on *Vocational guidance* was published in *Money Which*? September 1978.

Counselling services are not directly comparable with each other because they have different methods of working, different approaches and place the emphasis on different aspects of the services provided.

Some organisations will help you to market yourself (at a fee which is generally substantial, and may be based on your last salary). Good counselling firms concentrate on training in the techniques of self-marketing and job hunting, including interview behaviour, help with the preparation of a curriculum vitae, and personal counselling, advice and support until a satisfactory outcome has been achieved. No counselling service can guarantee to find you a job and any claims to do so are suspect.

If you decide to part with money to a counselling or self-marketing organisation, be very careful that you do not fall into the hands of a charlatan. You should discover to what other body a counselling organisation is attached; how long it has been in existence; the qualifications of its staff; the training in counselling which the counsellors have had. Try to persuade the counselling organisation to let you approach previous clients to get their comments. This is a delicate matter and not all counselling organisations will agree; however, it is worth trying.

Be sure you know the cost of the service and what you get for it, and how much work you are expected to do yourself. Only if you are entitely satisfied that you will get value for your money should you commit yourself.

Someone who is a member of the British Institute of Management can use its information service, which gives advice and information to its members who are seeking new appointments for any reason. An application form for membership of the BIM and details of criteria and fees can be obtained from Management House, Parker Street, London WC2B 5PT.

The BIM information unit provides literature on job search strategy and the legal aspects of job change and redundancy, information about pensions and contracts of employment, and on career counsellors and recruitment consultants. Members can have a session with a professional counsellor who can help to analyse the individual's strengths and weaknesses, identify possibilities and advise on job hunting techniques. The advice of the BIM counsellor may be that the individual could benefit from further professional advice.

organising yourself

Job hunting is a full-time job and needs self-discipline. You cannot afford to take more time off than when you were still employed. It is tempting to spend too much of your 'freedom' in family activities and on jobs around the house and garden which you have been meaning to get down to for months. Your priority must be the task of getting back into employment.

Try to estimate – realistically – how long it is likely to take you to find another job, based on a 'worst-possible' case. Face the fact that, unless you are lucky, there is a long haul in front of you. Coming to terms early with the likely time scale may offset depression as the weeks turn into months.

Establish a daily routine to ensure that you carry out job hunting activities before you turn to anything else. You and the family should discuss the new daily pattern and, where necessary, re-allocate tasks to allow for the change in roles. This is particularly important if your spouse is now going out to work instead of you. Where a husband is likely to be at home for a considerable period, the wife may be able to do something extra that she wants to do. It may be taking a job (which has obvious financial advantages) or herself taking a training or retraining course.

The job of getting a job requires considerable effort and readjustment for someone who has not previously worked at home. Try to set up an 'office' where you can work undisturbed, rather than using a corner of the dining table.

You must organise yourself and your time to make sure that the right things are given priority, that important things are not skimped, and that your energies are properly channelled. It helps to establish a routine by

- getting up at the usual time
- doing the planned work irrespective of temptations and distractions
- setting targets and keeping records (daily, weekly and monthly, for jobs applied for and offered) so that you can compare actual performance against targets.

Tedium may build up from the repetitiveness of the daily routine you have to impose on yourself. Having to write almost identical letters day after day, giving the same information over and over again, can become excruciatingly boring, but you must keep going. It helps the morale to get as much variety as possible into the regime, so plan to include different necessary tasks each day, and keep evenings and weekends free for other activities or relaxation, wherever possible.

Stay tidy in appearance; it is all too easy to slop about every day in jeans and house-painter's cardigan, until the wearing of a suit or dress feels unfamiliar. You may be called to meet a potential employer at short notice, with no time to smarten up. Do not put off getting your hair done or cut until just before you go to an interview – you may then be too conscious of your new hairstyle. Keep your interview clothes clean in case of sudden summons – it would be devastating to have only grubby clothes (motto: wash shirt or blouse straight after any interview, ready for the next).

Do your best to keep in trim and fit. When time allows, walk or cycle wherever possible. This advice may sound nanny-ish, but feeling fit and knowing you are looking presentable can – as well as making a good impression on an interviewer – keep up your own self-confidence and morale, which are assets to you in surviving a period of unemployment.

Keeping mentally fit is just as important as keeping physically fit. You may be missing the daily contact with colleagues at work, who kept your mind alert and active, and helped to set standards of work,

quality and output for you. You should find ways of keeping your mind exercised. If you have a friend in similar circumstances, try arranging regular meetings not for bar or coffee chat but to set each other mentally stimulating tasks. Attending night classes or other courses on work-related subjects also helps.

A programme has been launched by the TUC to encourage the development of a network of centres for unemployed workers throughout the country; some open part-time only, others on a full-time basis. The idea is to provide a focal point for unemployed people in a local community where they can get information and counselling from experienced trade union officers as well as a place to meet and combine forces to organise help and support for the unemployed in that area. The local branch of a trade union should know whether such a centre exists or is being established in an area, and a list of the current centres can be obtained from the TUC's unit on services for the unemployed at Congress House, Great Russell Street, London WC1B 3LS.

the state's help

The state's arrangements for helping people to get work are coordinated by the Manpower Services Commission, under which there are two executive arms: the Training Services Division (TSD) which administers training opportunity schemes (TOPS) and other training arrangements, and the Employment Service Division (ESD) which runs the nationwide chain of jobcentres and employment offices. The ESD has a separate service called Professional and Executive Recruitment (PER) for people at managerial or executive and professional levels, and also a specialist service for disabled people.

You can use these services while you are still working, as well as when you are out of work.

If you have not already registered at a jobcentre before leaving your job, register for employment on the first day of your unemployment. (Even if you are not yet claiming unemployment benefit, by registering you make sure that you are credited for national insurance contributions.) Going to a jobcentre will give you some idea of the system and what the job market offers.

PER courses

Amongst the services offered by PER are career review and development courses (in some places, called transfer of employment or TOE courses), lasting for two weeks, and shorter three-day courses on self-presentation. These courses are held in London and in some centres in other parts of the country once a month; there may be a short waiting list. The courses are free, and fares and an allowance to cover the cost of midday meals are paid. Details are available from your local PER office.

The courses are designed to teach participants the basic practical skills necessary for successful job hunting. They are conducted by professional consultants, who take candidates through the most effective procedure for applying for jobs, advise them how and what to find out about the organisation advertising a vacancy, and how to interview well. One day is spent on the marketing aspect of job hunting, the second on how to sell yourself (involving mock interviews, with post mortems and criticism by other participants) and the final day is for discussion of practical work and self-organisation.

The course can be very morale-raising, increase motivation and produce a renewed degree of confidence in someone who has become deflated and depressed by a series of unsuccessful applications.

curriculum vitae (c.v.)

One of the first things to do is to draw up your curriculum vitae (progress of life) or career history. This means assembling all the relevant facts about yourself, your career and abilities.

Preparing a curriculum vitae requires considerable patience, thought, introspection and self-criticism. An objective friend can be helpful and may point out omissions and inconsistencies and wrong emphases.

Although your c.v. relates to the past, it is designed to show, as briefly as possible, the benefits a company will get from employing you. It is a selling document.

Put down first of all every fact you can think of about yourself, then edit it into shape.

Your curriculum vitae should contain clearly separated sections, starting with personal details: full name, address, telephone number (day and evening), date of birth or age, marital status, children.

Then there should follow paragraphs to cover

1 your educational attainments
2 any career-related training you have had, giving the organisation responsible for the training, and indicating the purpose with a brief outline of the course; even part-time courses add grist to the mill
3 professional qualifications, and professional organisations to which you belong
4 work experience: start with your present job and work backwards,

giving the dates for each post held, the organisations you worked for, and the jobs you did in each. Do not leave out any period of time: a future employer will wonder how you spent an unmentioned year.

A last paragraph should add anything relevant to your personal particulars, special interests and skills, foreign languages.

Do not include references on a c.v. – you may want to alter your choice of referee for different applications.

more information

For a longer c.v., you can give more detailed information about all your industrial, commercial, technical, other work experience, the functions of management in which you have had experience, the responsibilities you have held, the skills or special knowledge you have acquired in management, marketing, finance, administration.

You can include fuller details about your non-work activities and interests such as sport and outdoor, cultural and intellectual (music, theatre, cinema, reading, chess). Remember that you may be asked about these pursuits at an interview, so if you say you like going to the opera, for instance, be ready to talk about one that you have seen recently and recall who sang the principal roles. Three to four leisure interests are enough: you want to make it appear that you have some time left to spend at work.

Put in also any local involvement you have (for example, scout group, church, parent-teacher association). But if you belong to any way-out organisation, political or religious group, it might be better not to include this, in case membership of such an organisation puts off a prospective employer.

A person who has had a long career and needs to get across what he has achieved, should not overdo the personal history. But for someone at the beginning of his or her career, personal details, especially education, are important information to give a future employer.

If you have rather a large number of jobs to record in relation to your age, or had some jobs for a very short time (or a job you would prefer to forget), you may want to manipulate the c.v. a little.

presentation

A curriculum vitae is important. Get advice about its presentation if you can – from your former employer's personnel manager, a recruitment consultant, staff at the local jobcentre and PER.

It is well to keep the presentation simple. Personnel managers and other 'sifters' prefer information to be clearly and simply presented, and might look a shade askance at anything oversmart. You must, however, consider what market you are hoping to penetrate: if you are trying to get into an advertising agency or marketing company, a smart glossy c.v. may be the right approach.

If possible, the c.v. should be typed, on one side of the paper only. If you cannot get this done by an expert typist, borrow a typewriter and type it yourself (it is worth the time and effort to peck it out with one finger – plus liberal application of erasing fluid or correction paper).

If you must leave it in your own handwriting, make sure it is legible, and write on white paper in an ink dark enough to be photocopied. It is irritating (and hence bad for your chances) for a personnel manager to have to work his way through a tatty c.v., on lined paper torn roughly from an exercise book, in poor handwriting and pale blue ink which cannot be photocopied for wider circulation.

Your curriculum vitae is a data bank for potential employers. It can be lodged with a recruitment agency, sent to contacts so that they can promote your interests in an informed way, and used by you for direct approaches and applications.

Having assembled the basic information about yourself, you should either be prepared to type out a separate c.v. for each application, highlighting relevant points for each, or have copies ready to send to any prospective employer and attach each time an expansion of the aspects of your career or personality that relate particularly to the job you are after.

applying for jobs

There are two basic aims: first to obtain an interview and then, as a result of it, to be offered a job.

The main routes, which should all be attempted concurrently, are

- applying for a job that is advertised
- placing your name on recruitment or employment agency lists
- applying direct to a company where there might be a vacancy ('cold canvassing')
- advertising yourself
- getting introductions through friends and contacts.

personal contacts

An unrealised asset is the number of people you have got to know in your personal life and through contacts built up during education and through work.

It is a good idea to sit down with your husband or wife, or someone else who has good knowledge of your background, and write down the names of all the people and organisations that come to mind, without at this stage evaluating them as potential sources of help or avenues of approach.

In brainstorming for a list of contacts, do not concentrate entirely on your recent employments: some of these contacts and ex-colleagues may be in competition with you and regard you as a threat. So, range widely – back to school and university, into non-work interests, family and friends (and their possible contacts, too). Other leads could be customers or suppliers with whom you have had dealings in other jobs. Cull names from your old address books and diaries. You will probably be surprised at how many names you have written down.

Then classify the list into people who might

- offer you a job
- introduce you to someone who might offer you a job
- give you practical advice
- be a good referee for you.

Neighbours and local friends should be told directly that you are looking for a job. They will learn about the fact of your unemployment sooner or later, so if you tell them yourself, it relieves them of the embarrassment of not knowing whether to talk about it to you. And they may know of possible jobs or have contacts in their own circle who can be useful to you.

references

Before you start applying for jobs, think of a number of people who will act as referees for you. Contact them personally first and ask if they agree in principle. The choice would normally be

- previous employer(s)
- work associates (colleague, customer, client)
- suitable friends (but not relatives).

You can give your bank manager, vicar, or a JP – the sort of person who, even today, has some standing in the local community. If you give someone's private address, it is a good idea to state his or her job or profession. In fact, it may be better to give their work address rather than their home.

Choose the referee to suit the application: certain people will be more appropriate for some jobs than others.

Write to or telephone them when you have used their name and say it was for such-and-such a job and would they please be prepared to say appropriate things about you when asked. Do not over-use any of them: he or she might get fed up – and also begin to doubt your competence after having given you a good reference several times in vain.

placing your name on agency lists

You should make use of the services offered by the various job-finding agencies: staff agencies, recruitment and selection consultants, the Employment Service Division of the Manpower Services Commission, and its Professional and Executive Recruitment service (PER).

at a jobcentre

At an ESD jobcentre, vacancies for jobs in the immediate neighbourhood, and also a selection from other districts, are displayed on notice boards, arranged according to the type of job. If you are interested in any job, tell the receptionist the reference number on the display card and ask if an interview can be arranged for you. A leaflet, *Finding the right job* (EPL 73), available at jobcentres and employment offices, gives advice on applying for jobs.

If you are disabled, you should ask to see the disablement resettlement officer, who will advise you about the special facilities available to help you find or keep work.

At some jobcentres, there is a 'job library' where you can browse through a wide range of occupational and job-related information. A visit there may help you decide the sort of job you want to try for. You can discuss your prospects and requirements with an employment adviser at the jobcentre, who will ask about your qualifications, the type of work you have done and jobs you might be suitable for. Where appropriate, you will be directed to PER.

with PER

PER was established to deal with jobs for people who are qualified academically or by experience for professional, administrative, managerial, executive, technical or scientific appointments.

You can enrol with PER by post, or by telephone or personal visit if you are near one of the district offices. There are about 30 PER offices throughout the country, with specialist branches in London and Birmingham for executive secretaries; addresses of PER offices are available from jobcentres and from PER head office, 4–5 Grosvenor Place, London SW1X 7SB.

You need to fill in a short form to enrol, and will be sent a booklet *A guide to successful job hunting*. You will be asked if you wish to attend a PER seminar, or to be considered for a course of training.

Every week you will be sent a copy of *Executive Post* which contains details of the jobs PER currently has on offer, divided into occupational areas, such as financial and administrative, sales and marketing management, computing, management services, scientific, technological. Each vacancy has to be applied for in the usual way either direct to the company or through the relevant PER office given in the advertisement. Applications may be 'refined' and short-listed and interviews arranged, and sometimes carried out, by PER consultants on the employer's behalf.

Your local PER office may ask you to fill in a more detailed c.v. to be submitted to prospective employers. Although PER ranks as the largest executive recruitment consultancy in the country, it can only offer jobs which employers have asked (and paid) PER to fill. So, the amount of help PER can give you depends on how closely your requirements match the kinds of job currently being handled by PER. The service is free to anyone looking for a job, whether at present unemployed or not.

at an employment agency

There are many employment or staff agencies where you can go to find out about jobs in the area and to be put on the agency's books for any suitable vacancy.

Commercial employment agencies often advertise in the press and display vacancies in their office windows. Although most specialise in temporary or short contract work, permanent positions can also be found through these agencies. There is some degree of specialisation – for instance, insurance, computers, clerical/secretarial appointments. Some agencies concentrate entirely on a profession or trade or particular type of job, such as nursing or catering.

There is no charge for registration or successful appointment; the employer normally pays a fee based on a percentage of the salary of any employee obtained through the agency. These firms make their living by satisfying employers who come to them for staff, so an agency's usefulness to job hunters is dependent upon what vacancies the agency happens to have on its books at the time.

Agencies also handle temporary jobs to cover a permanent employee's absence or for short-term extra work. If you are taken on on this basis, you are employed and paid directly by the agency, irrespective of the (always higher) sum the employer is paying the agency for you. When doing a temporary job, use the opportunity to learn about the organisation you are sent to work for, and then, if you want to, you may be able to sell yourself to them as a permanent staff member.

on a professional register

Some professional associations operate a recruitment bureau or register for their members.

For regular service men and women who have recently left the forces, the Regular Forces Employment Association has 40 branches throughout the UK (headquarters: 25 Bloomsbury Square, London WC1A 2LN). The Officers' Association (48 Pall Mall, London SW1Y 5JY) acts as a resettlement and employment agency for ex-officers of HM Forces. Both associations offer a free service of advice and help with re-employment.

A member of a trade union should tell his local union branch that he is unemployed, even though the union may already be aware of the situation. Some unions have a weekly mailing list for their unemployed members, of jobs that have been notified as vacant.

For a recent graduate, it may be worth going back to the university appointments board. A good source for graduates, and also for non-graduates, are the annual publications: *Directory of Opportunities for Graduates* (VNU Business Publications) and *Graduate Employment and Training* (Hobsons Press for the Careers Research and Advisory Centre, Cambridge), available at reference libraries.

recruitment consultants

Recruitment consultants (including PER) advertise jobs on behalf of employers, sometimes saying who the client is, sometimes not identifying the company. If the potential employer is not named, careful reading of the advertisement might give you some clue, even if only to the sector of industry involved. When you reply, try to show the relevance of your experience to the problems and opportunities of that industry. Think of likely companies in the sector and get to know something about them, so that you will be able to respond intelligently.

In some cases, the consultant merely acts as a post box; in others, he will sift and short-list candidates. In the first place, your response to the advertisement has to attract the consultant's attention as being someone who could do the job successfully for his client, so that he asks you to an interview.

An interview with a consultant acting on behalf of his client is an extra hurdle between you and the company. One difficulty is that you are unable to assess the 'chemistry' of the employing organisation, since it is only coming to you secondhand. It would be helpful to know whether the consultant has a long-term continuing relationship with his client. If so, he should be attuned to the organisation and able to convey its image so that you can assess it in relation to your background.

Having made your mark with a consultant, do not sit back and hope that he will do the rest: watch for any advertisements for jobs that his organisation may handle and ring him if you wish to be considered. And if you hear nothing for some time, remind him of your existence.

It is difficult to identify the scope of the various professional job-finders from their nomenclature: executive selection, career guidance, outplacement, recruitment services, and so on. Many such firms advertise themselves in the press, where the heading under which their advertisements appear may indicate what services they offer. By noting the type of jobs any particular recruiting agency or consultancy is advertising, you can get an idea of the market it deals with and whether this would be applicable to you and your circumstances.

Lists of recruitment organisations and individual consultants are included in publications such as *The Personnel and Training Management Yearbook and Directory* (Kogan Page) and *Kemp's Recruitment and Training Services Handbook*, available in public reference libraries; members of the Institute of Personnel Management can get an information note listing executive search organisations known to the IPM.

There is also the publication *The Executive Grapevine* which is a comprehensive guide to executive search and selection consultancies operating in the UK, giving information about each, including functions, industries covered, salary range and location of jobs found, fees charged, and a geographical list. It is available from the publisher at 79 Manor Way, London SE3 9XG (or ask your library to get a copy for you).

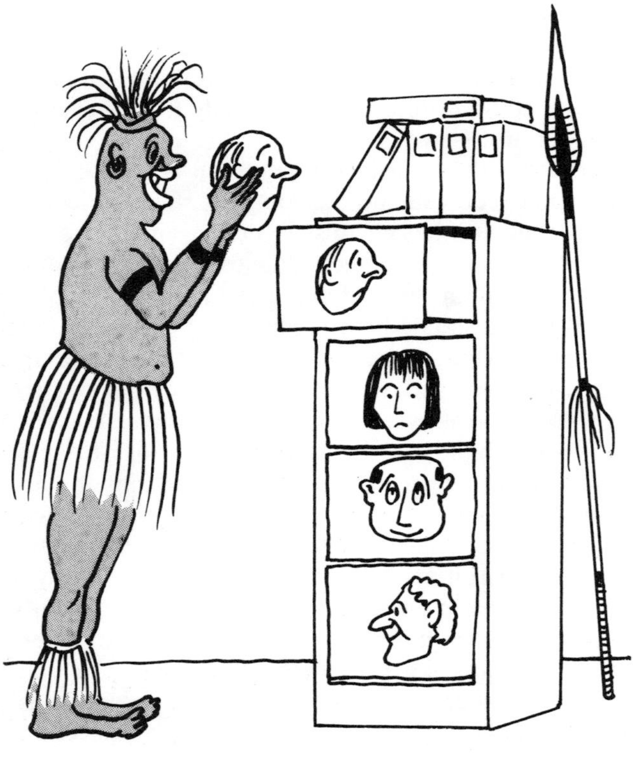

headhunters

A recruitment consultant who is approached by organisations when they wish to make a high level appointment is sometimes called a 'headhunter'. He does not necessarily advertise the jobs he handles, but makes direct approaches to individuals who might meet the specifications because of the work they are currently doing. You do not pay a fee to the headhunter, he gets paid by the organisations who use him.

Headhunters keep a file of people who have asked to be considered for jobs and who have sent in their c.v. Most headhunters receive hundreds of applications from individuals daily and yet, by the nature of their work, handle very few jobs. It is sheer chance if they happen to have a job to suit an individual at the time an approach is made. Nevertheless, they can be an avenue that is worth trying.

It is best if you can meet the consultant, so that you become an individual to him, and not just facts on paper. So, telephone to get a name to whom to send your c.v., and then ring again to arrange to meet him or her.

When you meet, try to establish a good rapport to show that you can handle relationships generally, as well as having the other qualities set out in your c.v. This may persuade him to recognise you as an asset to him – one that he can sell on to a client with mutual benefit.

the cold canvass

Provided you know the type of job you want, the sort of company you wish to join, and the geographical area, you can approach companies or organisations directly. Read newspapers and journals (in the library) carefully for news, to keep yourself generally up to date and particularly for

- information about business sectors and companies in which you may be interested
- notices of organisational changes and appointments which may suggest possible vacancies as a consequence or which may give you a name to whom you could make an approach
- announcements of company or office relocations or expansions which may create jobs in your desired area.

Not only the national press carries this sort of valuable opportunity information: it is important to read the local daily and evening press as well, for items about local firms, organisations moving into the area, local people taking up appointments. From your reading, you could build up files of notes, articles, press cuttings about relevant sectors and companies.

Other publications you may want to consult in the reference library include

Kompass Register (published by Kelly's Directories in association with the Confederation of British Industry)
volume 1 gives details about products and services and cross-refers to volume 2 which gives company information and location

Key British Enterprises (published by Dun & Bradstreet)
lists the 20,000 companies with largest turnover or prominent in their own line, alphabetically in two volumes

Kelly's Manufacturers and Merchants Directory
lists firms in alphabetical order and by classified trades

Who Owns Whom (published by Dun & Bradstreet)
volume 1 lists UK parent and overseas parent companies
volume 2 lists subsidiaries and their parent companies

Stock Exchange Official Yearbook
gives financial details of quoted companies and lists their directors

The Times Thousand
gives names of managing directors and chairmen, and figures for turnover and net profits of top companies

Current British Directories (published by CBD Research Ltd)
a guide to the various directories for trades and professions in the UK and elsewhere.

With information from these sources, you can choose the most likely companies to approach. Write to an individual director or personnel manager by name. Make sure that he or she is still in that position by ringing the organisation and asking the switchboard the correct title and name of the appropriate person.

Your letter should be brief. It should reflect whatever information you have acquired about the company, and should include some details from your c.v. which are relevant to the company's operations. The object of this letter is to persuade the reader that the firm needs a person like you and that you are an offer not to be missed.

Give the letter a couple of days to reach the right desk, and then ring up to suggest a meeting with the appropriate director or manager. If your letter has been passed on in the organisation, try to track down the person who is now dealing with it.

Do not be surprised if your approaches evoke a negative response – or none at all. Accept from the start that a high proportion of your cold canvassing may attract no immediate response. But your target company may be contemplating changes and the benefits you offer may crystallise their thoughts at least to the extent of 'putting you in the bank' for future use. Or the executive may have contacts outside his own company for whom your experience has interest, and may suggest other places to write to or may pass your letter on. In any case, such approaches are inexpensive, and give an incentive to do homework on a company or business sector which may bear fruit elsewhere.

into the public sector

Local government jobs are often advertised on notice boards in the town hall and public libraries, and in the publication *Opportunities*, a weekly guide to public sector appointments, available at most town halls and public libraries. Some of these posts, however, are filled from within the establishment and may already be earmarked at the time of being advertised. To find out about possible job opportunities in local government, write to the personnel officer of your nearest local authority, enclosing brief details of your qualifications and work experience or go in person to the town hall and ask about vacancies. (Some councils keep lists of potential recruits.) If you are considering working farther afield, you can get the addresses of all local authority personnel officers from the *Municipal Year Book*, which is available at most public reference libraries.

The Civil Service Commission is responsible for recruitment into the civil service. There are Civil Service Commission regional advisers throughout the country (listed in local telephone directories) who can be asked for advice and information on career prospects and how to set about applying. Booklets giving information about careers in the civil service at all grades are published by the Civil Service Commission, and are available free from Alencon Link, Basingstoke, Hampshire RG21 1JB and from Standard House, 28 Northumberland Avenue, London WC2N 5AL. The establishment officer at a government department in any area will have details of forthcoming vacancies there.

There are many grades of job in the civil service – clerical, executive, administrative, specialist (including economists, statisticians, scientists, engineers, lawyers, valuers, vets). Recruitment to a particular grade depends initially on educational qualifications. For most posts, selection is by interview (often two) before a board of at least 3 people, following, for some posts, quite stringent assessment. For example, candidates for executive officer have to pass a 3-hour written test (held once a year throughout the country), then two days of tests and exercises and interviews in London and a final interview before a selection board of 5 people.

New entrants to the civil service are given specific training for their job – many posts are filled by people without previous experience in the work. Anyone at or above executive officer level may be required to work in any part of the UK or, exceptionally, overseas.

through advertisements

Jobs are advertised in national, provincial and local newspapers, and in professional and technical journals and in periodicals. Monday is not a good day for job adverts in the national dailies, but it is a good day in some provincial papers. Some of the national newspapers concentrate on different types of job on different days of the week. When you have studied the papers for a while, you will be able to see the pattern of when to find jobs in, for instance, creative and media, education and administration, public sector, engineering and computers, general management, finance, law, marketing, personnel, printing and allied trades; jobs in the UK and overseas, jobs in the armed forces, the police and nursing.

If you are enrolled with PER, you will be mailed your weekly copy of *Executive Post* containing all the vacancies notified to PER during the week.

Call at the jobcentre regularly to look at the displays of vacancies, and to consult the staff. Usually the clerk who registered you has a special responsibility for you. Call regularly to see him or her so that he or she gets to know you and will associate you with any suitable job that comes in. Do not be content just to look at the display of jobs on cards.

Use the local reference library fully. Scan all the papers the library takes for vacancy advertisements; do not restrict yourself only to the ones you are familiar with. Include the periodicals, trade and professional publications. If you find that there are a lot of people wanting to get at the current day's papers, be content if necessary to scan them one day late – but never more than one day – and be sure to write off for any jobs straightaway.

If a publication which is relevant to your particular interest is not taken by the library, ask the staff if it can be acquired.

replying to an advertisement

Read and absorb the whole advertisement, and spend some time thinking about it before beginning to plan a response. If the organisation is named, go through your files for any relevant information.

Your reply should follow any instructions given in the advertisement, and quote the reference in full. If a curriculum vitae is requested, send one. Otherwise, write a letter saying why you think you are suitable for that job, and set out briefly the experience you have, and its relevance and potential benefit to the organisation. If you can go beyond the advertisement and refer to some aspect of the organisation or industry which has not appeared in it, do so. If you have only some of the experience or attributes required in the advertisement, be positive about them. Do not say what skills you lack or which requirements you do not meet. Time enough to deal with these aspects when you get to an interview – which is what your reply is aimed at achieving.

Remember that the letter of application is probably the only chance you have of writing about yourself – and it is yourself you are trying to sell. In the past, it was enough for an applicant to state what he had done in previous jobs for the employer to judge what he could do in the future. Nowadays, it is advisable to use a more forceful marketing technique:

- define what the employer needs ('. . . increase in sales . . .')
- state that you can satisfy that need ('. . . I can increase your sales . . .')
- provide proof of ability ('. . . because as sales manager of Bloggs and Co, I increased their sales by xx per cent . . .').

the letter

Good quality headed notepaper is a good investment. If you do not have any, make sure that you put your address and telephone number clearly on the first sheet. Keep a copy of the letter.

Your letter should be on the following lines:

name and department
organisation

reference no

your address
your telephone no

date

Dear . . . (*or* Sir/Madam)

1. (*this identifies the job*)
   Give the name of the post and when and where it was advertised.

2. (*this is the punch paragraph*)
   Put down your job experience over the last x years and what your responsibilities were – try to echo the wording used in the advertisement.

3. (*this is your back-up paragraph*)
   Mention previous experience (could include voluntary work) and other relevant information.

4. (*keep this one short*)
   Describe briefly your education and training, if relevant to the job and not too long ago, and give any professional qualifications.

5. (*this is an optional paragraph*)
   Give some personal details (and possibly some about your family), why you want to work in the area of the job (if it is far from where you are at present), how available you are for interview.

   I look forward to hearing from you.

Yours sincerely (*or* faithfully)

(*print your name underneath your signature*)

Do not offer the names of referees in an initial application unless asked to do so. But you can say 'I shall be pleased to let you have the names of referees if you would like them.'

Try not to exceed one sheet of paper, preferably getting it all on to one side – even a long and glorious career can be effectively condensed.

It is better to type your letter – so long as you can type it well: errors and crossings out will not act in your favour. Also, you can get more on the page if the letter is typed.

Employers and recruitment consultants often have many hundreds of applications for the same job. To make life simpler for themselves they often adopt the following routine:

1 reject all those which fail basic criteria (age, qualification)
2 reject letters that are too long (after all, they are only human and want a simple life)
3 reject letters on first glance that are scruffy, untidy, misspelt
4 sort remaining applications (sometimes only 25 to 50 per cent of the original) into possibles and 'sorry, no' piles.

To improve your chances of getting into the 'possible' pile, make your letter interesting by varying the basic format to suit your own individuality. Try to put yourself into the mind of the person who has advertised. Ask yourself what he will be looking for and order your response to suit him; leave some information out, if you think it sensible to do so. Never tell a lie – but there is no need to volunteer the whole truth.

This may apply particularly to information relating to your age. There is a tendency on the part of companies to stipulate a rigid age bracket for a job, which is then often used as a go/no-go gauge to enable the personnel manager or other recipient to sift replies rapidly and without having to think about some of them. Other companies pitch their requirements towards the younger age groups without any real thought of why or of the pool of experience from which they cut themselves off. So, if no age limit is given, or if one is given which could rule you out but you meet the other requirements, do not be put off – just omit all age information from your initial application. But remember to remove all dates from which age could be inferred – for example, relating to education.

application forms

Often, when you respond to an advertisement, you will be sent the firm's application or personal particulars form to complete. Even though you may have sent a c.v. with your initial reply, complete the form. It is tempting to fill in your name and then, instead of completing the rest of the form, write 'see c.v. enclosed/already submitted'. Doom. A personnel manager or recruiter is likely to be irritated by a response from someone who will not conform. The application form may have been designed to elicit relevant information in a set order appropriate to the organisation, so that in looking through many applications, comparison is easy. But there is no harm in sending a copy of your c.v. in addition to a completed form, if you want to.

Read the form through very carefully first, to find out exactly what is wanted. It is a good idea to write out on a separate piece of paper the information required and then copy it on to the form.

Some companies, and the civil service, stipulate that you fill in their application form by hand. This may be so that if you have to sit an examination, your handwriting can be checked to see whether it is the same as on your application.

Most application forms have a section which requires a response beyond the mere recitation of facts. This 'narrative' part of the form may have any of a number of headings, from the bland 'other information' to the more sharply pointed 'indicate why you are suited to this particular job'. Whatever the heading, it represents an invitation to sell yourself by highlighting particularly relevant parts of your experience, or the naturalness of this job as a step in your career development, or its relationship to your aspirations. Respond with thought and care and keep a note of what you write – it is likely to be pursued in greater depth at an interview, and it is better to be able to build on what you have written than to have to try and re-invent under an interviewer's gaze.

Keeping a copy of all your 'narrative' responses will save you from having to start from scratch for each application.

keeping records

Job hunting generates paper which will become a useless heap unless you organise it. Keep separate, preferably in individual files

- personal information: a copy of the c.v. (including the notes on which you based it) and additional information to be knitted in from time to time; copies of the 'narrative' section of application forms you have completed; details of people who have agreed to act as referees for you; degrees and certificates and other relevant documents
- details of each application: a copy of the advertisement; a copy of your application or annotated c.v. sent; subsequent correspondence; all the gobbets of information about the organisation that you acquire (for example, a copy of the annual report); notes of telephone calls; comments on interviews
- material about companies and business and industrial sectors culled from the press
- recruitment consultants and agencies contacted, with dates, so that a reminder can be sent or correspondence referred to.

It is a good idea to keep a master list of applications made, showing what stage each has reached. This enables you to avoid applying for the same job twice (often different advertisements for the same job appear within days of each other) and to sort out the 'dead' ones (but keep the file – the job may yet come up or another one with the same company).

Keep the files up to date and near the telephone, just in case you get telephone-interviewed. Anyone (including the children) likely to answer the telephone while you are out should be briefed and told to ask who is speaking, what is the name of the organisation or firm, what is the telephone number and extension and when can he or she be rung back. Keep a pad and pencil by the telephone so that calls and messages, with a note of the date and time, can be written down straightaway.

while job hunting

Many organisations do not acknowledge receipt of applications, although most will eventually tell you if you have not been selected. An advertiser using a box number may do so not only for anonymity but to avoid the chore of answering unsuitable applications or being bothered by people on the telephone.

Do not be surprised if you hear from only a small percentage of advertisements you reply to. Transfer the papers to your 'dead' file after, say, two months if no reply has been received.

There is a belief that for every 10 jobs you apply for you should get an interview, and for every 10 interviews, you should be offered a job. However true or false this belief is, getting a job is very much of a numbers game – the more applications you make, the more chance you have of success. Never let an opportunity pass by. It is not unknown for someone to be offered one job having been interviewed for a totally different job. So, every chance of exposure to potential employers should be exploited.

Try to have several possibilities going all the time. Even if one application seems to be going well, do not build all your hopes on it and relax efforts elsewhere. If it fails, you will have to overcome depression and regain momentum, so it is better to have other possibilities in train. Continue to

- send out application letters – in reply to advertisements
– direct to potential employers
- research the possibilities for direct applications (back to the library)
- collect company information in readiness for interviews (also at the library).

Make a job plan for each day, allowing reasonable time for meals and breaks, and try to stick to it. Be aware – and plan accordingly – that job hunting is expensive, particularly on a budget already suffering a salary drought. The postage and stationery alone will mount up. Also, domestic costs may go up. You will be at home more – using more tea, coffee and biscuits. The heating will probably be on for longer than normal.

Minimise other costs by planning. Allow enough time to walk (to the library, for instance) to save on petrol or fares. Make telephone calls after 1 o'clock, when they are cheaper than in the morning or, where possible, during the evening cheap rate times. Arrange interviews at times which will allow you to take advantage of cheap day returns.

looking for work in another area

The Employment Service Division of the MSC operates a job search scheme to help anyone who is unemployed or threatened with redundancy to look for a job in another area. So, if you are looking for work beyond normal daily travelling distance of your home, ask at your local jobcentre whether the job search scheme can help you. The main criteria are that there are no suitable jobs for you in your home area and that the employer in the other area has been unable to fill the job locally.

If the prospective employer confirms that there is a good chance that you will get the job, you may get a free return fare to go to an interview (provided, among other things, that the job offered is below a gross salary limit, currently £7308 per annum) and in some cases a grant towards overnight expenses.

You may even be helped to stay temporarily in the area where you are looking for work – where you will have to call daily at the local jobcentre or employment office to find out about vacancies and opportunities. You can only make use of these temporary transfer arrangements once in six months.

You must make a formal application for fare and subsistence money at your local jobcentre beforehand. Leaflet EPL 66 from any jobcentre gives general information about the job search scheme.

If you should get a job with a salary below the set figure of (at present) £7308 a year or £140 a week and beyond the daily travelling distance of your established home, you may be eligible for a grant or allowance under the ESD employment transfer scheme. Leaflet EPL 103 gives details of the conditions and what payments may be made (travelling expenses, transfer grant, household removal expenses, legal and estate agent's fees) and EPL 104 gives the rates.

a job abroad

There are sometimes as many advertisements for jobs abroad as there are for jobs in this country, and you may want to consider them seriously.

Working abroad can be

- a solution to the immediate problem of finding a job near home
- a logical step in your career or job experience
- a way of earning a lot of money quickly
- a permanent change in your life – by emigrating.

There are pros and cons, such as

PRO

the money is often better than in Britain (especially in the harsher environments where many expatriates can save part of their pay)

working abroad is a great educator and can do a lot to strengthen an individual's character

british employers generally regard a short period spent working abroad as an asset, if it is part of a logical career pattern

contracts are usually for one or two years so that you can be back in Britain rejoining the job system quite soon.

CON

cost of living there and inflation rate may be high (attractive salary may not be so attractive in practice) and there may be a liability for double taxation

work can be very hard and demanding, the work week long

accommodation can be very different from what you expect or are accustomed to

many jobs are 'bachelor' status only; when they are 'married', the change of environment may cause family problems

leisure time and facilities can range from bad to non-existent

there may be language difficulties, and problems with cultural and social adjustment

you may be in trouble if you really cannot stand the job or the place and want to come home.

If you decide to take a job abroad, you will need to obtain and check the contract of employment and conditions very carefully; consult your solicitor. Anyone who ordinarily works abroad, even for a UK company, is excluded from the scope of our employment protection legislation.

training

While you are out of work, you may want to take the opportunity to improve your chances (or yourself) and gain an additional qualification by taking some training or educational course.

A handbook to full-time and sandwich courses at polytechnics in England and Wales is published annually by the Committee of Directors of Polytechnics (309 Regent Street, London W1R 7PE) and should be available at reference libraries. A short guide outlining full-time and sandwich courses at the polytechnics is available free on request from the CDP. Information on part-time courses should be sought from individual polytechnics.

It is possible to study many subjects through a correspondence college. The Association of British Correspondence Colleges (6 Francis Grove, London SW19 4DT) will send a list of its member colleges and the subjects they teach, and the examinations covered. A list of correspondence colleges accredited by the Council for the Accreditation of Correspondence Colleges (an independent charity officially recognised by the Department of Education and Science) is available from the Council (27 Marylebone Road, London NW1 5JS). Both these bodies offer a free information and advisory service on all aspects of correspondence education.

TOPS courses

The government's Training Opportunities Scheme (TOPS), run by the Training Services Division of the Manpower Services Commission, offers free training courses for people who have been away from full-time education for at least 2 years and not had any other government training course within the last 3 years (a transfer of employment course does not count here).

Anyone aged 18 or over, whether unemployed or not at the time, can apply to go on a TOPS course, provided this is likely to lead to improved job prospects – not just to learn carpentry as a hobby, for example. You must be willing to take up employment in the occupation for which you train, although there is no guarantee of a job. The

courses range from bricklaying to electronics, from typing to management. No particular qualifications are required, but your suitability to the course you have chosen will be assessed – for example, someone who has no manual dexterity at all would be dissuaded from trying to be a typewriter mechanic or a watch repairer.

Information about what courses are currently available locally and elsewhere, and application forms, are provided at jobcentres and employment offices, where there is usually an employment adviser with specific responsibility for training.

The courses are held at government 'skillcentres', colleges of further education, universities, firms' premises. If there are no jobs locally in the skill you want to train for, you may have to go to another area to take the course you want to do. The courses last from one to 12 months, depending on the type of course.

The TSD leaflet N100 (N127 for disabled people) gives general information about TOPS courses (N100/9 covers the London region specifically and there are editions for other regions).

While taking a TOPS course, you are paid a tax-free allowance together with other benefits depending on whether you are living at home or away and on the number of your dependants. TSD leaflet N103 gives the current weekly rates of allowance for trainees and dependants.

A trainee's national insurance record is credited with contributions for the duration of the training course.

into the services

Someone who is prepared to be trained and undergo the discipline in one of the regular services should get in touch with the relevant careers information or recruitment office (listed in local telephone directories). There is a stringent assessment procedure for all branches of the armed forces and the police, covering physical aptitude and health (including eyesight and hearing) as well as personality and intelligence factors.

To discuss the possibility of taking up a career in the police, you can go to the recruiting office of the headquarters of the nearest district force (there are 43 in England and Wales, 8 in Scotland) or contact the Police Recruiting Department, Home Office, Queen Anne's Gate, London SW1H 9AT or the Police Division, Scottish Home and Health Department, New St Andrew's House, St James Centre, Edinburgh EH1 3TF. The preliminary application form sets out the minimum height for a police officer specified by the different forces (from approx 5ft 8in for a man, 5ft 4in for a woman). The Home Office recruiting department will supply brochures describing the career prospects and training schemes and salary scales in the police service. There is a special scheme of entry for graduates under the age of 30.

For the army, there are 175 careers offices throughout the country. You have a preliminary interview and medical check, before going to a selection centre for further information and assessment. The upper age limit for army entrants is generally 27 (or 29 for some specialist branches); you can enlist for 3 or 6 or 9 years at a time. The Central Recruiting Depot is at 5 Great Scotland Yard, London SW1A 2HJ.

In the RAF, opportunities exist for both commissioned and non-commissioned service, as aircrew or in one of the ground branches and trades. The maximum age of entry for service on the ground is 39 years; for aircrew it is much lower. Precise information about types of jobs and entry qualifications can be obtained from any one of the 71 RAF careers information offices, whose locations appear in local telephone directories. The central RAF careers information office (11 Lee Road, London SE3 9RQ) can provide general information about the range of jobs in the service.

Information about joining the navy, marines or WRNS, as an officer or rating, is obtainable from the RN and RM careers office at State House, High Holborn, London WC1R 4TG, and from any of the 62 naval careers information offices around the UK. There is a leaflet summarising methods of entry, requirements and training for the different categories, and separate leaflets explaining rates of pay, pensions and conditions and job opportunities and prospects in each branch of the naval services. The upper age limit for entry is 33 (RM and WRNS, under 29 years). The terms of engagement range from the right to give 18 months' notice after 18 months' service to a continuous service engagement of up to 12 years.

The police and members of the armed forces are outside the statutory employment protection provisions but the Race Relations Act applies; the sex discrimination legislation is operative for the police but not the armed forces.

life insurance during any period of unemployment

Many employers provide a considerable amount of life insurance for their employees. Some limit this to employees in the pension scheme, and there may be other rules regarding eligibility. If your former employer provided such cover, you may not have taken out insurance personally to provide for your dependants. So, if you leave one job and do not immediately move to another one which provides similar cover, your dependants may be inadequately provided for.

First, check with the employer you are leaving. It may be that the company's policy continues to cover you for a month after you have left, to help bridge just such a gap.

Maybe you can take out your own insurance with that employer's insurance company without evidence of health. But the insurance company may offer only a 'whole life' policy without requiring evidence of your health, not 'term' life insurance – which is what you probably need. Term insurance is cover for a few months or a year, say, and is very much cheaper than the annual premium for a whole life policy (which you continue to pay until you die or reach an agreed age, such as 65). A whole life policy eventually pays out, a term insurance policy is unlikely to have to – which is why it is so much cheaper.

interviews

Whenever you are asked to go for an interview, accept – even when you know that you do not want or (probably) will not get the job. It will give you practice, and reaction from interviewers may help you to clarify your aims and your strengths. Also, you will gain information about companies and their world which may be useful to you in the context of other applications.

If you receive a letter asking you to go for an interview, confirm straightaway. It is worth finding out, tactfully, if expenses will be paid. If the time or date is one that you cannot possibly manage, telephone, say why, and offer some alternatives.

You are not always told whether you will be seeing the personnel officer, head of department, managing director, chief clerk, works manager, supervisor, or whoever – nor the interviewer's name. If you can manage to find out, it is useful to know something about the man or woman who will be interviewing you and his or her role in the organisation.

Often there are two interviews, the first being to decide on a short list. So, concentrate during the first one on getting short-listed rather than on subjective details (such as how much holiday).

before the interview

Between being invited to an interview and the actual date, you should find out as much as possible about the company or prospective employer. The type of information to get hold of includes finding out exactly what the firm does and its range of products (if there is a showroom, go and look at what is in it), where the headquarters and branches are, how big it is, its profit history, reputation and competitors. Where appropriate, get a copy of the firm's latest annual report (this is generally available from the company secretary) and other publications, such as a copy of the company newspaper, or the employee report (a simplified version of the annual statement and report) or publicity material. If you go in person to collect the material from the main reception office, this will give you an opportunity to get a feel of the place – and you will know where it is.

The annual report may tell you something about employees – are numbers stable or fluctuating? does the chairman say anything about employee relations? Look at the chairman's statements to see if there is a discernible plan and consistent strategy. If there are comments such as 'a further review of the situation . . .', make a note possibly to ask about this.

Extel Statistical Services (37–45 Paul Street, London EC2A 4PB) provide up-to-date information on individual companies: activities, balance sheet, board members, capital and dividend record, profit and loss account, chairman's latest statement. This information is shown on cards for each company. The fee for a card on a british company is £1.95 (for a company not quoted on the stock exchange, £5.85). Some public reference libraries have Extel cards and information.

Look again at the key points in the advertisement – what is the job, why is it needed, what skills and qualities does it demand. Review again any other information (such as a job description) which you may have received.

Put yourself on the other side of the desk: if you were interviewing for this job, what would you be looking for? what would you regard as important areas to probe? what questions would you ask? what parts of the application form would you want to follow up? (not only the facts, but any aspects covered in the narrative parts of the form). Re-read your copy of the form of application you have sent.

Write down some of the key questions and prepare your answers: 'Why do you want this job?' 'What do you think you can contribute?' 'Why did you leave your last job?' or 'What are you doing in your present job?' Remind yourself of why there are any gaps in your c.v. and prepare the necessary explanation.

Preparing your responses is not only helpful to your interview performance but may genuinely help you to decide whether and why the job is attractive and important to you. If it is, your commitment will come through in your interview. Be prepared for questions relating to

• education and background
This is a warming-up subject which also helps the interviewer to begin to build his picture of you. Be ready to talk about your achievements and aspirations as a youngster, and avoid giving the impression that it is none of the interviewer's business

• special aptitudes
You may be asked about your qualifications and membership of professional or other institutions

• achievement – what have you done in your working life?
Remember to expand on what the jobs entailed – a product manager in one firm could have been doing quite different work from someone with the same job title in another company.
If you have ever stepped down or sideways in your career, or significantly changed direction, be prepared to explain why (and how it helped you in the long run).

• ambition
Expect the interviewer to want to find out whether you are likely to be content to remain in the post you are applying for or whether you would hope to rise within the organisation.

• health
You should not need to give medical details of illnesses at an interview, but if you have something wrong with you which might be regarded as serious (either by you or a potential employer), be prepared to disclose it if asked. You may have to agree to be examined by the firm's doctor, or to give consent to having your medical records made available.

Consider the questions you yourself want to ask, and those that the interviewer may expect you to ask. If writing things down helps your memory, make a note of the questions. But, whatever else you do, do not produce this list at the interview: nothing makes an interviewer's heart sink more quickly than seeing an earnest candidate produce a list of questions and show signs of wanting to trudge remorselessly through them all.

Think whether there are questions you will want to ask about the person you will be working for: how long has he (or she) been in his job? who does he report to? what developments have there been in his area of responsibility? have there been recent promotions, or transfers? why is there a vacancy now, and why is it being advertised rather than filled from within?

This sort of planning and preparing questions you will want to raise in the interview will enable you to bring them out naturally at the appropriate time. Knowing that you are well prepared will help to give you confidence.

It could help to get an angle on the approach from the other side of the desk if you look (in the public reference library) at the *Daily Telegraph Recruitment Handbook*, which contains advice and information to help recruiters to deal with applicants and find the best candidates.

The Institute of Personnel Management has issued for its members a recruitment code setting out the obligations of recruiter and applicant:

Recruiters' obligations

1 Job advertisements will state clearly the form of reply desired (for example curriculum vitae, completed application form) and any preference for handwritten applications.

2 An acknowledgement or reply will be made promptly to each applicant by the employing organisation or its agent.

3 Candidates will be informed of the progress of the selection procedure, what this will be, the time likely to be involved and the policy regarding expenses.

4 Detailed personal information (for example religion, medical history, place of birth, family background etc) will not be called for unless and until it is relevant to the selection process.

5 Before applying for references, potential employers will secure the permission of the applicant.

6 Applications will be treated as confidential.

Applicants' obligations

1 Advertisements will be answered in the way requested (for example telephone for application form, provide brief details, send curriculum vitae etc).

2 Appointments and other arrangements will be kept, or the recruiter be informed promptly if the candidate discovers an agreed meeting cannot take place.

3 The recruiter will be informed as soon as a candidate decides not to proceed with the application.

4 Only accurate information will be given in applications and in reply to recruiters' questions

5 Information given by a prospective employer will be treated as confidential, if so requested.

Copies of the code with additional comments are available free (if you send a self-addressed stamped envelope) from IPM, Central House, Upper Woburn Place, London WC1 0HX.

on the day

Decide what you are going to wear. Choose clothes in which you feel well turned out but comfortable and that are appropriate to the organisation and type of job. First impressions are important and you should aim not to distract your interviewer by extremes in dress – of either exoticism or scruffiness.

If you were not told in the letter, find out where to report, whether it is easy to find, whether there is a car park outside or a station or bus stop near by.

Set off for your appointment in good time and take a street map with you. If you are going by public transport, allow for it to be half an hour late. If you go by car, you may have to park some way from your destination (make sure you have change for the meter) and may have an unexpectedly long walk. Have the telephone number with you so that you can telephone if you are held up.

Aim to arrive at least 5 to 10 minutes early, or even earlier than this if you are going to a large building with several blocks. If you do not allow ample time and arrive late, this may not only upset your interviewer but will almost certainly fluster you and put you off your stride.

Arriving in good time will allow you to continue your preparations in the reception or waiting room. Greet the receptionist courteously: the interviewer might well ask her afterwards for her opinion of you – or she might volunteer it if she was impressed by you.

Look for product displays, and read any company literature which is available, such as marketing leaflets or house magazines. Try to pick out something that you can use in your interview to help establish rapport and indicate your interest in the organisation.

Notice the way the receptionist or telephonist deals with visitors or callers; listen to people talking to their colleagues or to visitors, such as representatives: what is the tone of the conversational exchange? is it courteous, helpful, humorous, brusque?

Review in your mind the questions you want to ask, and the answers you have thought out for the questions likely to be put to you. Use the waiting period to do what sports teams call 'psyching up'. The aim is to enable you to walk into the interview feeling well prepared, ready to talk, and able to take some initiative yourself. Have confidence – even experienced interviewers often find the start of a session difficult (they may be behind schedule or underprepared) and may welcome and follow a sensible opening gambit from the interviewee.

in the interview

Do not sit until invited – or at least until the interviewer sits down.

If you are offered tea or coffee, it may be wiser to refuse so that your concentration is not distracted. If the interviewer offers you a cigarette, it is acceptable to take one, or smoke one of your own. But do not be the first to ask if you may smoke – particularly if there is no ash tray in sight.

Make sure you get the interviewer's name right – but do not use first names. Find out what his or her role is in relation to the position you have come to discuss – for instance, sifting applicants? short listing? actually selecting? the person you will be working for?

Some interviewers remain practically silent and leave you to sell yourself to them; others follow a set pattern:

- giving details of the firm or organisation and the job
- asking questions designed to find out how well you fit the job requirements
- inviting you to ask questions.

You may be able to control the direction of discussion to your advantage to a certain extent. Try to generate a relaxed atmosphere by your manner and deportment.

Above all in an interview, listen. Listen not only to what an interviewer asks, but note how he receives your responses: watch for non-verbal indications of interest, agreement or boredom.

Listen to the interviewer's questions carefully and let him finish before responding. Do not make assumptions about what he is asking – answer the questions he actually asks. If you do not fully understand a question, ask him to repeat or amplify it.

You do not have to be too humble or docile: disagree if his views are not yours, or if he in any way misrepresents your views. You do not have to be brusque: "that is not quite what I said" can give you an opening to rephrase what you meant to be understood.

If your interviewer rambles, let him: you may pick up information about him or his organisation which will be useful to you. But do not ramble yourself. It is better not to answer at too great a length, with too much detail – nor too laconically. Do not produce examples of work unless asked.

A good interview should be as like a normal conversation as possible, and not just each participant taking it in turn to ask questions. So, try to develop your exchange into a conversation, rather than just questions and answers.

Not only will the interviewer try to find out if you are qualified for the job, but also to assess whether your personality fits in with those with whom you will be working. In any job, it is important to get on well with colleagues, and the interviewer will prefer someone who is pleasant and seems ready to communicate with other people at all levels.

Although there is an element of play-acting and self-salesmanship in any interview – and it is right that you should draw attention to your relevant strengths and attractions – it is important not to try to project what you are not. If you do not like, or are not good at, hard industrial relations, do not make yourself out to be a managerial toughie. If you are an authoritarian centralist and do not really believe in delegating decisions to a lower level, do not try to project yourself as a believer in an open management style. Even if you take in the interviewer, you would face problems with the job.

When you are asked to talk about yourself, it is unlikely that the interviewer wants any childhood reminiscences, so say something like: 'Shall I start from the time I joined Bloggs and Co?' He may reply 'No – I'd like you to tell me about your work at . . .'. Be prepared to fill in any part of your biography, and to give reasons why you left previous jobs. Remember that the interviewer relies for information and his judgment of you mainly on what you tell him. So be sure to tell him those things from your background that further your application, and do not dwell on awkward points. Try not to say anything negative in an interview – and never criticise your present or past company or colleagues.

The interviewer is looking for enthusiasm for the job and will expect you to discuss how problems that you are likely to meet in the job can be solved. If you ask questions, it not only indicates your interest but you can use the information you get in response at later stages of the interview: 'I think you said earlier . . .' and 'could we go back to . . .?' are openings to re-focus on something you want to talk about that will show up your knowledge and its relevance to the post you are discussing.

Do not necessarily wait for the interviewer to say 'Now, would you like to ask me some questions?' Introduce questions and answers yourself in any part of the discussion where it seems relevant to do so. This enables you to keep some of the initiative. If you leave all your questions to the end, they may sound artificial and not pertinent, and the flow of the interview may be broken. Your interviewer may be feeling 'Well, that's over' and may give you answers which you will not have a chance to re-cycle. Then, having answered, he may follow up with 'Well, if there's nothing else . . .', at which point you have entirely lost the initiative and will find it difficult to regain his attention and interest in anything you say.

An interviewer may lapse into silence: do not be led into trying to break it yourself and risk declining into mere babble. Wait politely, interestedly, for him to begin again or to tell you that the interview is over.

Before leaving an interview, you should ask what the next stage is, what the timing is and whether your referees are going to be approached. If you have other opportunities under consideration, you should let your interviewer know what time constraints you are under.

tests

For some jobs, a group of applicants is brought together and given a specific task – for instance, to organise the transport department or to open a new market in the Midlands – with a number of interviewers watching. Group exercises are designed to show how you work with people as well as how you set about solving problems.

In other cases, you may be given a project to complete, as a trial run of the work the job entails. This 'homework' may be given to you to complete before your interview, or afterwards, preparatory to being short-listed. As well as showing what you can do, the exercise may help you to decide whether the job is right for you.

panel interviews

In a panel interview, up to six people may be interviewing you. You may not be told exactly who everyone is but try to find out. Remember at least some of the names and find an opportunity of using them (for instance, when the person asks you a question). Most of us love to hear our names used and this applies to panel members.

The most influential person may not be the chairman of the interviewing group – this usually becomes apparent at an early stage. It is unlikely that the group work as a team like this often, and they are therefore unlikely to be well coordinated. Usually, each person sticks to his or her own area of questioning; they may have set questions to ask each applicant.

For some appointments, it is a statutory or professional requirement that the job is advertised and applicants interviewed by a selection board. In some cases, this is just a formality and the decision has already been as good as taken.

Where it is a local government post, there may be an interviewing panel of four people, probably consisting of chief officer (who asks most of the questions), chairman and two councillors. This panel will then report back to the relevant committee, recommending a couple of candidates. These short-listed candidates will then have to appear before the full committee, with the original panel. The panel may run through a number of the same questions again, so try to remember their names and your answers.

When you are being interviewed by a panel, make eye contact with each member; watch for non-verbal communication between them. Try to identify if one member is pre-eminent and worth making particular responses to.

Some interviewers or panels may try to put you under stress in some way: for example, by asking several questions in quick succession without pausing for an answer. Respond quietly to those you can recall, and ask for others to be repeated: 'I think there was something I haven't answered' turns it back to the interviewer who has to remember what it was, and its importance.

If an interviewer tries to needle you in any way, perhaps by ridiculing your response, or misrepresenting what you have said, do not react by getting angry. Correct him firmly, or re-state your own point coolly (to the point of chilliness, if you feel it appropriate) in order to show that you can cope with arguments, can handle pressure and have the courage of your convictions.

Sometimes an interviewer or panel chairman may ask right at the beginning of an interview 'If you were offered this job, would you accept it?' Do not fluff – answer 'Yes' or, if you are not sure 'Almost certainly but there are some things I still want to know, and I am hoping that this interview will give me the information I need'.

Some jobs, including local authority and academic ones, if offered must be accepted or rejected on the spot. The logic behind this is that the panel conducting the interview is responsible for the appointment and would find it inconvenient to re-convene; so, should the preferred candidate refuse, they go through the list until someone does accept the post that day.

interview expenses

Where expenses you have incurred will be met, you should detail them on a sheet of paper with your name, address and date of interview, making it simple for your interviewer to authorise and pass on for payment.

If you know beforehand that the interviewing organisation is not going to pay expenses, you may be eligible for the return fare to the interview from the Manpower Services Commission's job search scheme (described in leaflet EPL 66 available from jobcentres).

salary and other questions

If no actual salary figure has been given, try to get the interviewer to indicate the likely salary or at least the salary range. Be prepared to negotiate. Take your present salary as a starting point, and add something on. Be realistic. Do not aim too high and price yourself out of the market. On the other hand, you have to be able to meet your living needs, and remember that if you pitch your aim too low in relation to what you have been earning, potential employers may wonder 'What is wrong with this chap?'.

Ideally, you should not have to earn less at your new job than you did at your previous one, unless there is the certainty of promotion in the near future. But you should balance the disadvantages of taking a step backwards in earnings against the benefits of having a job and being in an organisation's potential promotion stream. This is particularly important if the organisation in question is one in which you know you can rapidly begin to make a contribution. Look at the 'packet' as a whole – including pension, fringe benefits, prospects. Try not to say anything that will preclude an offer: it is easier to negotiate with an offer in hand than without. If the company will not pay as much as you would like, consider taking the job with the proviso that your salary is reviewed within a few months.

There are some questions which it may be inappropriate to ask at a first interview, but you could ask the interviewer whether you will have an opportunity to discuss these items later.

The first interview, for instance, may not be the time to ask about

- hours and working conditions
- salary review practice
- opportunities for training
- holiday entitlement
- pension scheme
- benefits (expenses, car, insurance)
- overtime.

But if you are offered the job, you should have information on all these points while deciding whether to accept.

after the interview

When you leave an interview, do not be surprised that you have the let-down feeling that comes after any period of concentration or effort.

Try not to have high expectations. A good interviewer will not indicate a judgment or conclusion until he or she has had time for reflection and comparison. A bad interviewer may be enthusiastic and encouraging – to every candidate.

It will help you to remember the important points, including names and facts about the firm – as well as your own reactions – if you note them down immediately after the interview and put the note with the relevant papers.

Contact your referees and tell them what sort of job it is that you are under consideration for; this will enable them to respond intelligently rather than with a set-piece reference.

Analyse the interview in order to make use of the experience in subsequent interviews or if you are called to a second interview for that job. Did you put your relevant strengths and experiences across adequately? Did you handle awkward questions satisfactorily? (If so, you can plan to use a similar response again. If not, how can you do better?) Did you ask all the questions you had planned? Were the answers helpful, and did they give you any pointers about the job or organisation which need further thought? Did you obviously say the wrong thing at any point? (If so, can you tell why?) Did the interviewer's approach show you how he saw the personal requirements for the job? What did you feel about the 'chemistry' of the interview, or the organisation?

Remember also that just as you were trying to sell yourself, by emphasising your relevant strong points and glossing over or avoiding your weaker ones, so your interviewer, too, may have been doing the same in respect of the organisation and the particular job.

You may want to make some further checks about your prospective employer – both the organisation and the individual you will be working for.

Look through your contacts list again and see if you can find anyone – employee, former colleague, customer, supplier – who can give you any useful information that you lack, or about which you have slight unease, particularly about the intangible aspects: relationships, business practices and reputation, product reliability.

At the end of the week of your interview, it may be a good idea to write a letter to the interviewer saying how much you enjoyed meeting him or her and the discussion you had, and confirming your interest in the job.

There may be a long, long pause before you get any notification, so do not destroy the papers. It could be embarrassing to be offered a further interview or the job when you no longer have all the details.

being offered a job

The decision to accept a job should, if possible, be taken coolly in an objective state of mind, preferably not immediately following the tense atmosphere of an interview. So – unless, of course, everything about it fits your requirements exactly – if you are offered a job at the end of a first interview, resist the temptation to say 'yes' straightaway, and give yourself time to review the situation.

If you still have other possibilities at the time you are offered one job, try to find out when you will hear the result of the others before you accept or reject the first offer. It is quite acceptable to ring up and ask whether a job you have applied for has been filled.

When you are offered a job, you are in the strong position of knowing that they want you, and you can therefore negotiate the best deal for yourself. Some employers have rigid salary structures and have little room for negotiation. Most, however, have considerable flexibility and can be persuaded to give you more than they originally proposed, to ensure that you come and work for them. Remember that all future improvements are based on what you negotiate at the beginning. Employers generally respect a person who bargains positively in his or her own interests – and is therefore just as likely to do the same for the business when an employee.

The more important you are to a company you move to, the more likely you are to be able to negotiate, for instance, special pension arrangements.

pension scheme

You should ask for all the information you require about the pension scheme, including when you will become eligible. You are legally entitled to information once you have the right to be a member of the scheme, but there is no reason why you should not be provided with details when being offered a job.

If you want information before you accept a job, try to contact the firm's pensions person directly rather than getting the information from the person who interviewed you for the job. But it might be a good idea to ask the interviewer to give you an introduction to the administrator of the firm's pension scheme (this may be the personnel officer or company secretary, or there may be a company pensions manager).

Otherwise, the pensions manager might be reluctant to talk to you about the scheme if you ring him up out of the blue. If you need more information, you should find out from the administrator of the scheme who the trustees are and ask one of them to provide the information.

information

There is likely to be a handbook giving information about all the terms and conditions and benefits of the prospective new employer's pension scheme.

The basic facts you should find out include

- is the scheme compulsory or voluntary? (if voluntary, carefully consider any alternative)
- is it in or contracted out of the state scheme?
- do employees make contributions?
- can you transfer funds from your previous pension scheme?
- how soon after joining the new firm can you join the pension scheme?
- is there any life insurance cover? (if not, or there is a gap between being a member of the previous and the new scheme, you may want to get interim cover).

The 'benefits' and the formulae used to work out what an employee will get vary widely from pension scheme to scheme. Some pension schemes, particularly those that have been modified over a number of years, have extremely complex benefit structures, and you will have to seek advice from the pensions administrator or manager.

Published information on various aspects of occupational pensions is available
from The National Association of Pension Funds, Sunley House, Bedford Park, Croydon CR0 0XF, including
Code of practice on provision of information to members of pension schemes (price £1.50)

from The Trades Union Congress, Congress House, Great Russell Street, London WC1 3LS
a guide to occupational pension schemes (1980 price 50p)

free from social security offices or by post from DHSS (Leaflets), PO Box 21, Stanmore, Middlesex HA7 1AY
NP 32 *Your retirement pension*
NI 196 *Social security benefit rates*
NP 23 *Occupational pension schemes (guide for employers)*

free from Company Pensions Information Centre, 7 Old Park Lane, London W1Y 3LJ
How a pension fund works
How to understand your pension scheme
How changing jobs affects your pension
Pensions for women

free from Occupational Pensions Board, Apex Tower, High Street, New Malden, Surrey KT3 4DN
OPB 1 *Pension rights on changing your job*

The Occupational Pensions Board can be asked for advice on whether the rules of a scheme comply with the legislation on occupational pensions. It can help with certain pension problems, but has no power to intervene in any disputes between scheme members and the administrators and trustees.

state pension
Part of an employed person's national insurance contributions go towards providing a basic retirement pension from the state at the age of 65 if a man, 60 if a woman. You get the full amount of pension only if sufficient national insurance contributions have been paid or credited. An additional, earnings-related, pension is available if you have paid an employed person's standard rate national insurance contributions on eligible earnings since April 1978 (not for any periods during which you paid the lower rate contributions for members of contracted-out pension schemes nor for any period paid at the special reduced rate for married women and widows).

The state basic pension is not affected by changes of job so long as the necessary contributions are made or credited.

occupational pension
Many employers run their own pension scheme to provide in addition what is known as an 'occupational' pension for their employees when they retire (at an age specified by the employer). Some such schemes are voluntary, and an individual employee can opt not to join, relying on the state pension and his or her own savings to finance the years of retirement. Others are compulsory for employees who come within the scheme's eligibility conditions. Some employers have more than one scheme, for different categories of employee.

Some employers themselves provide all the money for their pension scheme. Most, however, require contributions from members of the scheme, to be deducted from their salary, the rest being put in by the employer. The money is put into a trust fund, with trustees responsible for the investment and administration of the scheme.

There are two categories of occupational pension: not contracted-out are those schemes whose members also make full national insurance contributions to, and are eligible for, the full state pension (basic pension plus additional earnings-related) and contracted-out are those whose members make the lower rate national insurance contributions to, and are eligible for, the basic state pension only.

contracted-out

For a scheme to be allowed to be contracted-out, it has to provide a pension at normal retirement age which is at least as good as the state additional pension would be (and a widow's pension of at least half the husband's).

The amount of the state additional pension is $s \div 80$ for each complete tax year from April 1978 in which you will have been paying contributions (this you cease doing at state retirement age). For someone retiring after April 1998, the 20 best 's' figures count.

$s =$ the amount of your salary between set salary limits; these change every year (in 1981/82, the lower and upper earnings limits are £1404 and £10,400 per annum).

To take account of inflation, the 's' figure for each year is revalued in line with national average earnings.

The part of a contracted-out pension equivalent to the state additional pension is known as the guaranteed minimum pension; this is increased by the state in line with national average earnings once the pension is in payment. The maximum pension of a member of a contracted-out scheme is two-thirds of final salary plus the state basic pension: a member of a non-contracted-out scheme can get that overall maximum plus the state additional pension.

A money purchase scheme does not qualify for contracting out of the state pension scheme.

money purchase schemes

Most employers' pension schemes provide members with a pension based on the product of years in the scheme and final pensionable salary. There are, however, other methods of providing pensions, a common one being the money purchase method.

In such a scheme, the member's contributions, usually plus most or all of the employer's contributions, are earmarked for the individual. The individual member is entitled on retirement to a pension and/or a lump sum based on the total of these contributions plus compound interest. In some schemes, the employer makes an additional contribution which is not earmarked for individuals but is used to provide an underlying guarantee, specific extra benefits, or extra benefits which are at the discretion of the trustees of the scheme.

leaving a pension scheme
When you leave an employer's pension scheme, you may have one of three options: taking a refund, having the pension deferred or preserved, transferring to a new scheme. Not all of these will necessarily be open to you.

refund
The law allows a refund of your own contributions only (never the employer's) provided that you are under the age of 26 or have been in the scheme less than 5 years when you leave (if you transferred funds from another scheme, your period of membership in that scheme counts as part of the 5 years), provided that the scheme's rules allow refunds. And anyone can have a refund of contributions made before 6 April 1975 when they leave a scheme, if the scheme's rules allow it. Some schemes pay out interest on the contributions, some do not.

If you opt for a refund of your contributions and the scheme was a contracted-out one, the scheme you are leaving 'buys' you back into the state scheme, by paying the difference between the lower rate national insurance contributions paid while you were contracted out and the full rate contributions that would have been paid had the scheme not been contracted out. The refund you get is usually reduced by the amount needed to provide your share of the contributions required to buy you back into the state scheme.

Tax at 10 per cent has to be paid on the amount of refund you get. Most schemes take this out of the refund before the member gets it, rather than out of the general funds of the scheme.

deferred pension
If you decide on a deferred pension (also called a frozen or paid-up or preserved pension), the scheme you are leaving will provide you with a pension at the normal retirement date (and may provide benefits

for dependants if you die before reaching this age). Generally, the amount is fixed at the time you leave the scheme, based on your pensionable salary at the date you leave and the number of years you were in the scheme, and does not necessarily increase to take any account of inflation.

Alternatively, a scheme may use the member's contributions (and in some schemes also a contribution from the employer related to the member's contributions), plus interest before and during the deferred years, to provide the pension.

If the benefits provided by the scheme you have left improve, these improvements may or may not be applied to your deferred pension. It is likely that this will not be decided until the improvements are introduced. You would be well advised to keep the explanatory booklet about the firm's pension scheme and any announcements circulated while you were an employee, or sent at a later date. Keep the scheme rules and a letter explaining your entitlement (ask for this if it does not come automatically) with your will. It could be worth reminding a previous employer's scheme of your existence every, say, 5 years, and whenever you change your address – just in case the fund winds up and trustees or administrator want to contact you. About every 5 years also ask whether any changes in the rules have been introduced which will affect your pension.

If the old scheme was contracted-out and the new one is not, the scheme you are leaving has to provide in your deferred pension at least the guaranteed minimum pension. To take some account of inflation between when you leave and the state retirement age, the scheme can undertake to increase the guaranteed minimum pension element by a fixed percentage each year, which the state will then undertake to top up if necessary, or the scheme can undertake to increase the guaranteed element in line with the increase in national average earnings. Under the rules of some schemes, the non-guaranteed element of the deferred pension gets eroded to pay the increasing guaranteed element.

transferred pension

The scheme you are leaving may be prepared to pay into the scheme of your new employer the present value of your deferred pension. This, referred to as its 'transfer value', is the amount of money (worked out by actuaries) the scheme you are leaving would have to set aside now in order to provide a pension for you at normal retirement age (or benefits at earlier death, if these are part of the scheme rules).

The scheme that accepts the transfer may invest the transferred lump sum separately (or at least earmark it as a separate investment) and convert it into a pension at whatever annuity rates apply when you retire. Or the transfer value may be integrated into the new scheme, 'buying' you a number of years in it. It is probable that you will 'buy' in the new scheme only a small fraction of the years that you had in your old scheme. This is because the transfer value is likely to have been based on your pensionable salary at the time of leaving, with no allowance for salary growth until retirement age. If you have actually worked 20 years in your first job and are offered 10 added years in your new job, that is probably quite a good bargain if you are confident that you will stay in your new job and that your salary will have more than doubled by the time you retire; but not so good if you accept 10 added years and after one year in the new job you move on again. At that stage, your salary has probably risen little or perhaps not at all. So, anyone who settles for 10 added years probably ought to try to negotiate an underlying guarantee of at least the amount of the frozen pension he could have received had he left his pension behind as a deferred pension payable from the first scheme.

If both the old and the new schemes are contracted-out, and you want to transfer the pension from the previous scheme, the new scheme will have to agree to increase the guaranteed minimum pension element in line with the increase in average earnings to retirement. This can well cost more than the transfer can earn when invested in the scheme – which explains why contracted-out schemes are often not willing to accept transfers from other contracted-out schemes. However, the schemes may agree to leave the guaranteed minimum pension element in the old scheme and transfer the non-GMP element to the new.

public sector transfer club

Most public sector schemes, and also a number of schemes in the private non-industrial sector, are members of the Public Sector Transfer Club. Schemes in the club agree to use a standard calculation for the transfer value when someone leaves a scheme and a standard calculation for the number of years to be credited when someone joins a scheme from another one.

If you think that one or both of the schemes you are concerned with may be a member, ask the pensions manager. Find out also whether the scheme is in the 'inner' club (including the civil service, local government, health service, teachers) or in the 'outer' club (most of the nationalised industries' schemes).

The club rules are designed to avoid as far as reasonably possible (bearing in mind the different benefit structures of each scheme) a loss of pension entitlement when changing jobs. Schemes which are members of the outer club will make and receive transfers in accordance with club rules only if the other scheme is a member of the club (inner or outer). Members of the inner club normally transfer to and accept transfers from any other scheme, whether inside or outside the club, on the club's favourable terms.

If you transfer your pension and both schemes are in the club (inner or outer), your pension rights are likely to be relatively unchanged as a result of changing jobs, so that is one aspect of changing jobs you do not have to worry about.

private pension plans

Pension schemes designed for the self-employed are offered by insurance companies. They can be taken out by anyone who is not in pensionable employment, or is not a member of an employer's pension scheme even if he is eligible to be. Private pension schemes are subject to Inland Revenue rules (as occupational schemes are); premiums paid for such a scheme are free of tax provided they add up to less than 17½ per cent of your net earnings. A good scheme may be a good way of saving for retirement for anyone who is not eligible for an occupational scheme.

Anyone with the choice of a private or an occupational scheme should remember that the employer as well as the employee contributes to an occupational scheme and therefore that there is more money available. Also, most employers' occupational schemes are now based on final salary, so if you stay in the scheme until retirement, your pension is more or less going to keep up with inflation, at least up to the date of retirement, while with a personal pension plan there is no such guarantee.

Nevertheless, there can be circumstances when it would be better to opt for a suitable private pension plan when membership of an occupational pension scheme is not a condition of employment. (You would also have to contribute to the state additional pension scheme – you cannot contract out on the basis of a private pension scheme.) *Money Which*? reported on *Personal pension plans* in December 1980.

You can get information and advice about private pension schemes from financial consultants and brokers. A personal recommendation is often the best way to find such an adviser. Or you could write for the names of their members in a particular area to the professional bodies:

The British Insurance Brokers' Association
130 Fenchurch Street
London EC3M 5DJ

The Corporation of Mortgage, Finance and Life Assurance Brokers
88 Victoria Road
Aldershot
Hampshire
GU11 1SS

The Society of Pension Consultants
Ludgate House
Ludgate Circus
London EC4A 2AB

A consultant or broker either charges you a fee or keeps the commission he receives from the insurance company or other organisation who arranges the pension for you. As a first step, you should always get clear and agree the basis on which you will be charged for the broker's or consultant's services.

what will you get in the new scheme?
Most occupational pension schemes that are contributory and contracted-out of the state scheme, provide a pension based on the number of years within the scheme and final pensionable salary.

The following are some points to watch for:

• what is the salary basis?
The pension will be based on the final pensionable salary. Each of the three words 'final pensionable salary' may be defined differently in different schemes. For instance, salary is not necessarily annual salary at the date of your retirement; final may mean the average of the best 3 consecutive years' salaries in the last 10 years. Pensionable salary may exclude overtime and bonus payments, and may be offset by the state basic pension.

• what is the formula?
The pension may be 1/60th of final pensionable salary for every year worked for the employer, or 1/80th, or 40/60ths for ten or more years' service with the employer.

• is state pension counted in?
Some employers' schemes take account of the state basic pension, and provide, for example, 'a pension which, when added to the state basic pension, will equal 1/60th × final pensionable salary for each year of service'.

With such a scheme, check carefully just what you will get over and above the state pension, and how the occupational pension will be affected by increases in the state pension. It and the state pension should both go up year by year – the employer's in relation to your increasing salary and years of service, and the state pension in line with inflation.

• pension increases after retirement?
Ideally, you want your pension to be index-linked to keep pace with inflation. Index-linked pensions are common in public sector schemes,

very rare in the private sector. Some schemes do not commit themselves to any increases in pension to take account of inflation, others guarantee percentage increases – of 3 per cent per year, say. Many schemes, or employers directly, increase pensions on a discretionary basis instead of, or on top of, a fixed increase. Discretionary increases, however, depend on the company's continuing policy and prosperity.

• cash lump sum on retirement?
Some employers' schemes provide both a pension and a cash lump sum. Most of those which provide only a pension allow some of the pension to be converted to cash (the jargon is 'commuted'). The lump sum may be 3/80ths of final pensionable salary per year of service and 120/80ths after 40 years – or this much may even be provided after 20 years. This lump sum is counted into the calculation for the Inland Revenue limit of two-thirds of final salary.

• what is the scheme's retirement age?
In the majority of schemes, the normal retirement age for men is 65; most of the others have a retiring age of 60. For women, it is the reverse – for most schemes 60, the exceptions mainly 65. In most schemes, provided the employer agrees, you can retire earlier, or later, than the normal retirement age – but with a smaller, or larger, pension.

The snag with an early retiring age is that when the pension is based on the number of years in the scheme and on final pensionable salary, both will be lower. Also, if you retire before a scheme's normal retirement age, the scheme usually takes account of the fact that your expected life (and pension) span is longer than if you had retired at the normal age, and so the annual pension has to be smaller. It is not uncommon for the pension to be reduced by ½ per cent for each month that you retire before the normal retirement age.

If you retire later than the scheme's normal retirement age, it is likely that you will not have to make any further contributions to the scheme. Nevertheless, with most schemes, the amount of pension you get will be more (perhaps ¾ per cent per month more, depending on the scheme's rules). The reason for this is that the money available for your pension at the normal retirement age can earn interest until you do retire – and also by then your expected pension span will be shorter.

• what happens on death after retirement?
When a pensioner dies after retirement, most schemes provide a widow's pension. This is usually 50 per cent of the member's pension

at the date of his death, increasing (if at all) at the same annual rate. A pension for a widower or other dependant is less common.

In some schemes, a member can provide more for his widow or other dependant on his death by electing to take a lower pension payable to himself.

Many schemes guarantee to pay a member's pension for so-many (usually 5) years after retirement: if the member dies after, say, 3 years, the remaining 2 years' pension, at the rate applicable at the date of death, will be paid out either in monthly instalments or as a lump sum (usually paid at the discretion of the trustees, to avoid capital transfer tax). Guarantees differ from scheme to scheme.

• what happens on death in service?

The majority of schemes provide both a pension for dependants and a lump sum if you die while still a contributing member of the scheme. These benefits (the jargon is 'death in service' benefits) differ considerably from scheme to scheme.

Some schemes provide a pension for widows only, some do provide for widowers, some for children, some for any one adult dependant. A common benefit is a widow's pension equal to 50 per cent of the pension the man would have got had he retired on the date he died. Others provide a widow's pension of 50 per cent of the pension the man would have got had he lived on to retirement without any further increases in salary but taking into account the years up to the date of the normal retirement.

Some schemes, on the death of a member, provide a lump sum for one person or to be shared by a number of people. The recipient of any lump sum is at the trustees' discretion. (This avoids any liability for capital transfer tax and delay which follows if the money goes into the estate.) Usually, a member expresses a wish about who should receive such a benefit and the trustees take account of these wishes when exercising their discretion.

Some schemes provide a dependant's pension in addition to a (smaller) lump sum. A large lump sum will be a more attractive benefit to someone with older dependants (or without any dependants) – you may have adult children whom you would like to benefit from your membership of the scheme in the event of your death. On the other hand, the younger you are and the more children you have, the more attractive will be a scheme with pensions for dependants.

choosing

If you have a choice between preserving the pension in your last employer's scheme or transferring it to the new employer's scheme, seek the opinion of both schemes' pension administrators before coming to a decision. You need to know the assumptions on which the transfer value is calculated by your previous employer's scheme and on which the transfer value is being utilised by your new employer's scheme. Assess not only whether the financial difference between deferring and transferring is of benefit to you, but any difference between the two schemes in such areas as retirement date, provision for post-retirement increases, provision for pension for a spouse and any other benefits that may be relevant to you.

Your new employer's pension scheme may not give you personally as much benefit from the transfer value of your previous pension rights as your old scheme would have done. If you think the basis of the benefits in the new scheme could be improved, ask the trustees and/or your new employer to review the basis. In the meantime, you should arrange to keep your rights in your previous scheme in the form of a deferred pension, and delay any transfer until you are satisfied with the terms. Once you are satisfied, do not delay – transfers often take months to arrange, even when all goes well.

accepting a job

It is ironic but you may well find that after weeks, or months, of disappointments, silences, rejections, you are suddenly offered several jobs within the same week. The choice may be agonisingly difficult: whether to take the highest salary regardless of what the job entails in the way of travelling, environment, the work itself, or whether to opt for a lower salary in more congenial circumstances, or to go for security. You may be forced to accept second-best because of financial or other pressures. Even though jobs are at a premium in the present economic climate, it is important to think through the personal and practical consequences of accepting an offer and of rejecting it.

Go through an offer letter and be sure about the terms under which you will be employed, particularly the starting salary and job title, and whether the contract is fixed term or subject to mutual notice.

You should get clarification and information on various formal and practical details. Many of these will be in a letter or document of appointment, or perhaps in a company handbook or staff notes. If you have not been given full details of terms and conditions, ask the employer to provide these:

- name of employer
  (the firm or organisation, rather than your individual boss)
- date when employment starts
  Will there be an overlap with the previous incumbent? if so, for how long? Is there any induction period, or any opportunity to visit before you actually take up your post?
- job title and scope
  Is there a written job description? If there is a grading system, what grade is the job? Who is the job holder responsible to?
- any probationary or trial period
  If there is a probationary period, how long is it? Can it be extended for any reason? How will you know whether you are seen as making satisfactory progress? Is there a salary increase or other benefit on successful completion of probation? During the probationary period, what notice are you entitled to? and are you able to be a member of the pension scheme and have life insurance cover?
- notice period
  How long notice has to be given on either side?

- place or places of work
  Are you required to work elsewhere (abroad, for instance) as part of the job?
- salary
  What is the basic and any ancillary payment such as commission, bonuses, overtime (how and when paid)? How is salary reviewed? is it a general annual review on a set date, or a review on a date specific to you (e.g. anniversary of the date of starting)? are increases based on merit, service, incremental scales – or on the individual asking? if incremental, what are the steps and when are increments paid? When and how can you move into another salary grade?
- hours of work
  What is the basic working week? and the normal daily hours? If it is more convenient (e.g. because of travelling), can you vary the daily hours? Does a formal scheme of flexible working hours operate? if so, on what timetable? Does overtime become payable at any point? if not, and you work more than standard hours, can you claim a meal or travel allowance and/or take time off in lieu?
- grievances
  If there is any dispute between you and your boss, what is the procedure for settling it? Does the organisation have a formal grievance procedure? How do complaints progress through the hierarchy and to what level?
- redundancy
  What terms would apply?

In the event of later dismissal or redundancy, some of these points can be crucial to any settlement or compensation.

Other important points which you should get information about from the personnel manager or your immediate boss include

- membership of the pension scheme, and what this entails and will provide for you
  Can you transfer in from another employer's pension fund? Is it possible to pay additional voluntary contributions? Is life insurance cover provided as part of the scheme?
- the normal retirement age, and options for earlier or later retirement
- holidays
  What is the holiday entitlement in a full year? in the current year for you? what about holidays already arranged? Are there limitations

on how holidays can be taken? for example, do you have to take part in summer, part in winter? can you take it all in one go? can you carry over holiday entitlement from one year to the next? What are the arrangements for holiday pay?

- sick leave entitlement and pay
  Is there more than the state benefit? Will you be eligible for regular health checks? Is there group membership of a private medical insurance scheme? if so, does it include members of your family?
- any 'perks' that come with the job, such as
  - car supplied by the employer or part expenses of your own paid (if a car is allocated, what are the arrangements covering private use?)
  - private medical insurance premiums paid for
  - clothing provided or paid for
  - loan facilities (for season ticket, mortgage, children's education)
  - free or subsidised meals, or luncheon vouchers
  - professional subscriptions

  bearing in mind any tax liability that may arise on such perks, particularly if your salary is over £8,500 a year
- help with any expenses incurred by taking up job
  (special equipment or clothing; on moving house, removal and legal costs, estate agent's fees, temporary accommodation)
- expenses generally
  How are you reimbursed? against receipts, or in the form of standard subsistence and travel allowances? What is the mileage allowance? What class of travel are you entitled to claim for?
- trade union
  Is membership of a trade union encouraged/a condition of employment? Can you keep your present union membership? or is there a union which is regarded as more appropriate to your level/type of job? Will your subscription be deducted automatically from your pay?
- staff association
  If there is a staff association, what are its activities and benefits: is it a social or a negotiating body? what is the subscription?

If you decide to accept the job, write an enthusiastic letter of acceptance.

starting

Knowing initially about practical arrangements can make the taking up of a new appointment easier and less anxious and wasteful of time. Many firms who employ a number of staff produce a staff handbook or staff notes, which should set out the normal arrangements within the organisation. If you overlap for a period with the person whose job you are taking over, he or she may be a good source of information about daily procedures and protocol, and the hierarchy of the organisation: who reports to whom and the structure for consultation or decision-making.

It would help to know about the general administration such as

- secretarial services
- the telephone (how to use the internal system, whether personal outside calls are permitted, how calls can be made or received after normal working hours)
- the filing system
- any library or information service
- time-keeping requirements (method for recording time spent)
- tea/coffee and meal breaks
- car parking facilities
- any groups within the organisation a staff member can join: sports, keep fit, drama, music, bulk buying, subscription schemes.

Your own assessment of the set-up when you were being interviewed should enable you to know what style of dress will be acceptable or required, and the general tone of formality or informality among the staff.

Make sure you get told about any in-service training that may be available, either full-time, one-off or part-time, and whether there is any financial help or incentive attached. If you work in your own time for a further qualification related to your work (taking, for instance, a correspondence or Open University course), will the organisation offer you any financial assistance, or study leave with or without pay? You may be bound to make known any freelance extra-mural activities, even voluntary work.

In due course, find out tactfully how to go about getting promotion – if you want to move up and on. Who can you talk to about career development? how will your performance, and suitability for promotion, be assessed and by whom?

Once you have definitely accepted a job, and there are no outstanding questions about terms and conditions, write to any other organisations to whom you have applied and tell them that you have accepted another post. Thank them for their courtesy and interest. Remember that you might want to apply to them again at some time in the future.

additional voluntary contributions

Your expected pension is likely to be less as a result of changing your job than if you had stayed in your current job. Bringing your pension up to a level you think you will be able to live on, means investing for a good return later. If you are prepared to save regularly for your retirement, and not to draw on these savings, it could be a good investment to make additional voluntary contributions (AVCs) to your employer's pension scheme. Once started, you will have to continue to make these payments for at least 5 years (or until you leave or retire) in order to benefit from tax concessions. Only in exceptional circumstances would you be allowed to stop.

One reason why additional voluntary contributions can be so attractive is that, like normal contributions to the scheme, they are deducted from your pay before calculation of tax – the equivalent of tax relief at your top rate of tax. There is an Inland Revenue limit on overall contributions to a pension scheme: you can pay in up to a total of 15 per cent of your annual taxable earnings. So, if you pay, say, 4 per cent as an ordinary contribution to your scheme, you can pay up to 11 per cent as an additional voluntary contribution. Generally, these savings accumulate tax free and you will get benefits based on their value when you retire. You may have some choice about the type of benefit they are used for on retirement.

If you are interested in making AVCs and your new employer's scheme does not allow for them or offers a return less than you think it should, discuss the matter with the employer or one of the trustees of the pension fund – there is no reason why an attractive AVC scheme cannot be set up for you.

Gone
to a
new
job

Being an employee

There are statutory requirements on any employer and any employee, stipulating rights and obligations on both sides.

The most important consequences of being an employee are that

- you can claim statutory employment rights including redundancy payment, remedies for unfair dismissal, time off work for specified events
- your employer has to meet stringent safety requirements
- your employer must be insured against claims by you for personal injury
- both you and your employer must pay national insurance contributions.

Many of the provisions of employment protection legislation apply only to people who are employees. Some employers and employees have attempted to avoid the duties thus imposed by entering into arrangements purporting to confer self-employed status on the 'employee'. Generally, however, the fact that an agreement treats the worker as an independent contractor is by no means conclusive if other indications point the other way.

Whether you are an employee or an independent contractor is, ultimately, a question of fact. There are some accepted indicators:

- whether another person has the right to say what you do in your job, when you do it and how you do it
  (Thus, a chauffeur always under orders is an employee; a taxi driver is an independent contractor since how he drives his passengers from one place to another is for him to decide.)
- whether you are part and parcel of the firm's business or organisation (For example, a newspaper columnist is an employee, a freelance contributor is not.)

You are an employee if

- you do not take any risk as to the firm's profit and loss
- you are paid a wage, rather than a lump sum or commission
- you work regularly for the employer, rather than as a one-off job or on different terms every time
- the firm has the right to select, suspend or dismiss you.

Some types of employment have special arrangements as far as entitlements to statutory rights are concerned. The main ones are

- crown servants (which includes all civil servants): their terms are generally covered by civil service department regulations and it is a moot point whether they have a contract at all
- the police: they are employed on terms laid down in the Police Act
- apprentices: their contract involves the employer agreeing to teach the apprentice a trade, profession or business and to maintain him or her. Although generally included as employees by statute, there are certain modifications in an apprentice's rights to claim redundancy payment and unfair dismissal remedies.

Booklets on aspects of employment legislation published by the Department of Employment are available (free) from employment offices and jobcentres, and from the Department of Employment public enquiry office, Caxton House, Tothill Street, London SW1H 9NF, and from citizens advice bureaux.

the contract of employment

Any contract is simply an agreement whereby one person accepts another's offer and gives cash or consideration in kind. It is rare that a contract of employment is wholly in writing.

Some terms of a contract of employment are implied by the common law, others by statute, such as the Employment Protection (Consolidation) Act, and others arise by custom and practice (that you may have an annual holiday at a particular time because that has always been the case). Some of the terms will be expressly agreed between yourself and your employer; the more senior you are, the more bargaining power you will have in this respect.

In companies with trade unions, most of the provisions about pay, pension rights and sickness are likely to be derived from the collective bargain which the union has negotiated with the employer. You will be covered by that bargain even if you are not a member of the union which has done the negotiating. Some industries are subject to joint industrial councils or wages councils and the council's orders will be incorporated automatically into the contract of employment.

It is important to distinguish between a contract of employment and other sorts of agreement.

written statement

Where there is no formal written contract, employees who work over 16 hours a week have the statutory right to be given a written statement of the main terms of their contract. This must be received within 13 weeks of starting work.

A written statement must include

- the identity of the employer and employee
- the date when the employment began and whether any previous service counts as continuous
  (This may have important implications for the right to, for instance, redundancy payment)
- the title of the job
  (This does not mean a full job description and may, for instance, simply say 'clerk' or 'typist')
- the rate of remuneration or the method of calculating it
  (This is important because redundancy and many other payments depend on the pay to which you are entitled)

- whether the remuneration is to be paid weekly, monthly or at some other interval
- hours of work and normal working hours
- entitlement to annual and public holidays, and holiday pay (This should be in sufficient detail to be able to calculate entitlement for accrued holiday pay on leaving)
- provision for incapacity to work due to sickness or injury, including provision for sick pay
- information about pensions and pension scheme (if any)
- the amount of notice of termination that the employee must give or be given or, if the contract is for a fixed period, the date of the end of the period.

Where there are no provisions relating to the items that must be stated, 'none' must be declared by the employer.

In addition, there must be a written note about disciplinary rules. This should specify a person in the firm to whom an employee can apply if dissatisfied with any disciplinary decision taken in relation to him or her, and how to apply.

In the additional note, the employer must state whether a contracting-out certificate, under the Social Security Pensions Act, is in force.

The employer, instead of giving each employee an individual written statement and note, can refer (in writing) to documents to which the employee has a reasonable opportunity of access while at work, such as works rules or handbook, booklet(s) about pension scheme, notices permanently displayed. A notice on a notice board referring to a collective agreement may be sufficient, for instance.

If no written particulars have been given to an employee at the end of 13 weeks, he or she may refer the matter to an industrial tribunal. The tribunal has power to determine what particulars the written statement should have included.

Any subsequent changes that are made to your terms of employment affecting matters set out in the written statement must be notified in the same manner within one month.

A booklet *Written statement of main terms and conditions of employment* (no 1 in the Department of Employment employment protection series) includes an example of a form of written statement.

A written statement is not, however, your contract of employment – it is merely some evidence of some of the terms of the contract.

implied terms of contract

The general rule is that even where there is no express provision in a contract of employment, some terms which are reasonable and necessary are implied. For instance, you, as an employee, are obliged

- to obey any lawful and reasonable instructions
  Your employer cannot, however, make you do things you are not contracted to do, such as to work overtime 'voluntarily'.
- to take reasonable care
  If you were to drive your employer's car negligently, you could be made to pay for any damage caused.
- to work and generally cooperate with your employer
  A work-to-rule may infringe this.
- to be trustworthy in handling your employer's property
- to account to him for all money received in the course of employment
- not to use any confidential information or trade secrets gained in the course of your employment, even after your contract has ended.

An employer may seek to go beyond this implied term by inserting an express term in his rules or contracts preventing solicitation of customers or engaging in competition for a period of time after you have left his employ. Contractual terms of this sort in 'restraint of trade' are illegal unless they are reasonable and in the public interest. Reasonableness depends on the area in which the former employee is not allowed to operate, for how long, and how directly such activity would affect the former employer's business. If your contract includes such stipulations, get advice before accepting.

An employee is expected to give the employer the benefit of inventions made in the course of employment. Detailed rules about this are in the Patents Act which accords the employee-inventor a right to claim a fair share of the profit of an invention of 'outstanding benefit'. Under the Copyright Act, the employer has the copyright of any material written in the course of your employment; you, however, generally own the copyright of what you write in your own time.

The Equal Pay Act implies into every contract of employment a clause that all terms and conditions will be the same for men and women. The Act sets out the ways in which you can make comparison with a person of the opposite sex about pay, terms and conditions of your job.

Implied terms include the employer's duty to give supervisors reasonable support in dealing with subordinates; not to make persistent and unwanted amorous advances to members of staff; and to treat the employee with due dignity and respect.

pay and hours

To qualify for employment rights, you must work a certain number of hours each week. You are covered if you have a contract which normally involves 16 hours or more per week. It does not matter if you, in fact, work less than 16 hours in a particular week because of, for example, sickness. You are also covered if you actually work 16 hours even though not contractually obliged to do so.

On the other hand, if you normally work between 8 and 16 hours weekly, you qualify only when you have been so employed for five years or more by the same employer.

If you work for less than 8 hours a week, you do not come under most of the employment protection legislation.

hours of work

There are no general maximum hours of work laid down in this country, and statutory intervention has been haphazard. Hours of work are restricted in some limited sectors – for example, baking, sheet glass making, shops and, most recently, lorry driving. Women in factories must not be made or allowed to work over 48 hours a week or more than 9 hours a day, to start before 7 am or finish later than 8 pm (but a factory may gain exemption from these provisions to allow for overtime and shiftwork).

time off for public duties

An employer must allow employees who hold certain public positions reasonable time off to perform the duties associated with them. He need not pay the employee for this time. These time-off provisions apply to an employee who is a justice of the peace, a local councillor, a member of a statutory tribunal, of a regional or an area health authority or of a water authority, or who is on the governing body of a local education authority educational establishment.

The time off is only for attending meetings and executive functions. The reasonableness of the time off depends on all the circumstances, in particular the amount of time required to carry out the duties; the amount of time off the employee has already had; the effect of the employee's absence on the employer's business.

time off for union activities

An official of a trade union recognised by the employer for the purposes of collective bargaining must be accorded time off with pay to perform any duties concerned with industrial relations. Officials include shop stewards and conveners, and other union representatives.

The pay to be granted is what the official would actually have received if at work at the time.

Duties include collective bargaining with management; informing union members about negotiations; interviewing members about grievances; appearing on behalf of members at an outside body – for example, an industrial tribunal. It does not include attending group

committees formed merely to swop information nor going off to TUC courses about the general state of the economy – there must be some relevance to employer/employee relations. But an official has a right to paid time off to attend training courses approved by the TUC or his own union, provided these are directly related to his union duties at his employment.

Safety representatives appointed by the union at the particular workplace are also entitled to reasonable time off for their activities.

All trade union members have the right to reasonable time off without pay to take part in activities of their union. The term 'activities' is rather wider than duties, and can include attending union meetings and voting in union elections.

workless days

There is an implied obligation for an employer to provide work for someone whose earnings vary according to performance and attendance (for example, on piece rates, being paid on commission); similarly, to provide work for an employed performer or writer who would lose the opportunity to gain in reputation if not allowed to work.

Most employees have a statutory right to receive a payment up to a stated maximum in respect to workless days. You are covered by this provision if you

- work 16 hours or more a week, and have had at least 4 weeks' continuous employment with the same employer

or

- work 8 hours or more a week but less than 16, when you have had at least 5 years' continuous employment with the same employer.

The 'workless' day must be one on which you would normally have worked and you did not work because your employer's need for the kind of work you do has lessened or some other occurrence has affected the normal working of the employer's business. This may be because of a fall in orders, lack of raw materials, power failures, bad weather, or the bankruptcy of a major customer. You cannot claim a payment, however, if

- your workless day is due to a strike affecting any employee of your employer or an associated employer
- the employer has offered you suitable alternative work and you have unreasonably refused it

- you do not comply with reasonable requirements imposed by the employer, such as clocking in every day or holding yourself available for work if necessary
- you have been hired for a period of 12 weeks or less.

At present, the maximum for such a guarantee payment is £8.75 per day.

In any period of three months, you are entitled to a guarantee payment for as many days as you normally work in a week, up to a maximum of five. So, at present, the maximum you can get is £8.75 × 5 = £43.75 even if you are workless during many more days than five in the three months.

Guarantee payments are subject to tax and you cannot also claim unemployment benefit in respect of a day for which you have received a guarantee payment.

Many collective agreements provide that in the event of short-time or lay-offs due to factors outside the control of employer or employees, contractual pay should continue. This is likely to be for a higher amount or for more days than the statutory guarantee payment – but you cannot get both for the same day(s).

Booklet no 9 in the Department of Employment employment protection series deals with *Guarantee payments*.

lay-off and short-time

Any week in which an employee gets no pay because there is no work for him or her to do, counts as a week of lay-off.

A week counts as a week of short-time if, because of shortage of work, the employee gets less than half a week's pay for that week.

After having had three days of no work (not necessarily consecutively but at least the first two within the same week, the third within 8 weeks), you may be able to claim unemployment benefit for any subsequent days on which there is no work for you to do.

An employee may qualify for redundancy payment if he (or she) has been laid off or been kept on short-time for four consecutive weeks, or for a period of six weeks out of any thirteen. The employee must give written notice within four weeks of the period coming to an end that he intends to claim redundancy payment. If the employee does not hear from the employer within seven days, he can leave and claim redundancy payment (if necessary, through the industrial tribunal).

However, if the employer thinks there is a reasonable prospect that he can offer not less than thirteen weeks' full-time employment, starting no later than four weeks from the date of the employee's notice of intention to claim redundancy, he can serve a counter-notice (which he must do within seven days). If the work then does not materialise, the employee can complain to the industrial tribunal.

continuity of employment

To qualify for many employment rights, an employee must have been continuously employed for a specified period: for example, to claim redundancy payment, 104 weeks.

Usually a week in which you are not covered by a contract of employment breaks continuity. Even if you then go back to the same employer, you would have to start a fresh 'continuity'. But if you work even one day of a week, that week counts and the statutory period of notice also counts.

Continuity can be maintained when you change jobs within an organisation, provided that this is specified in your written statement of employment. Your service can be continuous with two employers provided that

- the business in which you are employed is transferred as a going concern to another person or company
- by act of parliament, one corporate body takes over from another
- your employer dies and his personal representative or trustee keeps you on as an employee
- there is a change of the partners who employ you
- you are engaged by an associated employer (an employer who is a company of which the other, directly or indirectly, has control or both are companies of which a third, directly or indirectly, has control).

A break after which the employment is taken up again may not affect the continuity of the employment if the period of not working was due to

- sickness or injury (for not more than 26 weeks plus any contractual sick leave period)
- pregnancy and maternity (if absence not more than 26 weeks)
- circumstances in which, by arrangement or custom, you are regarded as continuing in employment (for example, your employer 'lends' or seconds you to another employer but considers himself still responsible for you)
- temporary cessation of work.

Any week of lay-off or short-time due to an employer being unable to provide work still counts towards continuity of employment.

A strike cannot be included as temporary cessation of work. While strikes do not break continuity completely, any week in which a strike takes place (even if it is only a 10 minute walk-out) does not count towards the calculation of continuous service. If you are locked out by your employer, however, the week will count.

Where a contract normally involves employment for 16 hours or more a week, but is temporarily varied so as to provide for between 8 and 16 hours' work, continuity is not broken provided the reduction does not go on for more than 26 weeks and you then go back to a contract of 16 (or more) hours a week.

calculation of pay

It is important to know the rules for calculating a week's pay in order to work out entitlement on a claim for redundancy payment, pay in lieu of notice, maternity pay, medical suspension pay, a protective or basic award on unfair dismissal.

The calculation depends primarily on whether you have normal working hours fixed by your contract of employment. If you do, the calculation depends on whether you are a

- time worker – where your pay does not vary according to the amount of work you do in the time worked: your week's pay is that received for the normal working hours
- piece-worker, shift worker or roster-worker – where the pay varies with the amount of work done or according to the time of day or week when the work is carried out: an average of weekly pay is taken for the previous 12 weeks.

Overtime can be counted only where your contract obliges you to work, and your employer to provide, a certain fixed amount of overtime. If you do overtime but your employer does not have to give it to you by contract, the calculation of your week's pay would be based on your basic contractual hours even though you have been working many more hours a week.

If you do not have normal working hours and your hours fluctuate from week to week – for example, an outdoor sales representative paid wholly by commission – a 12-week average of earnings is taken.

In calculating pay, benefits in kind such as free accommodation and travelling allowances, are disregarded. Contractual bonuses and regular supplements are, however, included.

The Department of Employment booklet no 11 in the employment protection series deals with *Rules governing continuous employment and a week's pay*.

low pay

There is no national minimum wage in the UK such as exists in many other countries. There is, however, some protection for certain low paid sectors of the work force.

Nearly three million workers are covered by 33 wages councils. Originating in 1909, the first councils, then known as trade boards, were established in what were 'sweated' trades; later councils were created for other trades in which wage bargaining machinery was either weak or non-existent. Today, there are wages councils for, among others, retail distributive trades, catering and clothing manufacture and also two agricultural wages boards (administered by the Ministry of Agriculture, Fisheries and Food). Wages councils have powers to fix statutory minimum rates of pay, holiday pay and entitlements, accrued holiday pay and other terms and conditions. Employers are required to display, on their premises, official notices setting out current wages regulations so that workers may know what the current rates are and what changes have taken place. If you think that your employer is not observing the provisions of a wages order, you should contact the wages inspectorate, a branch of the Department of Employment, whose duty is to enforce all wages orders, and who can, if necessary, bring on your behalf an action for breach of contract in the county court. You can recover for underpayment of wages for as far back as six years.

Little known are the Truck Acts (1831 to 1940) which deal with the manner in which wages should be paid to manual workers. (The name is nothing to do with truck drivers but comes from the french word *troquer* = to barter.) The first statute in 1831 was aimed in particular at the abuse of 'tommy shops' whereby workers were paid in tokens to be exchanged at the company store for goods. The evangelizing employers of the last century thought they were doing the right thing by giving people groceries instead of money – which they feared would be spent on liquor before it ever reached the homestead.

equal pay

The Equal Pay Act sets out the ways in which you can make comparison about the pay, terms and conditions of your job with a person of the opposite sex doing like work. The other person must be the previous incumbent of your job, or someone employed by the same (or an associated) employer at that place of work or at another place with similar terms and conditions of employment.

To determine whether the work is the same – or at least broadly similar – find out whether there are any different duties in your contracts of employment and, if so, whether they are performed to some significant extent; also, whether there are differences of practical importance in relation to the terms and conditions of employment.

More formally, comparison may be made through a job evaluation study. Such schemes are often jointly agreed between management and trade union. The evaluation usually breaks a job down into such basic elements as the effort, skill and decision needed to perform it, and gives points for each element. If the job evaluation study rates the jobs as equivalent, the respective terms of employment must not show any discrimination.

An employer has a justification for paying a man higher wages than a woman if he can prove that there is a genuine and material difference (other than sex) between his case and hers. An employer cannot point

to market forces – that the man would not have taken the job if he were offered less than the woman – as a justification for the difference in pay: the employer's case must relate to the characteristic of the particular person.

The main differences which have been held to be genuine and material are

- longer service
- age
- higher qualification for the job
- different locations (women who worked for the NAAFI in Nottingham could not claim parity with men similarly employed in London)
- an agreed grading scheme based solely on personal factors
- 'red circling': where a long-serving employee is given a lower grade job – for example, because of ill health or old age – but still receives the previous rate of pay.

A complaint about non-equal pay can be made to an industrial tribunal at any time while employed or within 6 months of leaving the employment in question. The industrial tribunal can order the employer to pay up to two years' arrears of pay – that is, two years preceding the date of your application to the tribunal.

Another way in which the Equal Pay Act seeks to ensure equality is that you can complain if your collective agreement, wages council order or pay structure is discriminatory. This is a collective matter and any complaint must be taken up through your trade union or made to the Secretary of State for Employment, who will probably refer the matter to the Central Arbitration Committee. The CAC has power to extend to men and women any provision presently applying to one sex, and to raise women's terms and conditions to the appropriate male rate.

There is a Department of Employment booklet *Equal Pay*, a guide to the Equal Pay Act.

your pay

Most employees have a statutory right to receive, at the time of each payment, a written itemised pay statement. This must include the following details:

- the gross amount of the wages or salary
- the amount of any fixed deductions and the purposes for which they are made: for example, contribution to the firm's pension scheme,

subscription to a staff association or trade union; also payments under an attachment of earnings court order for payment of fines or maintenance contributions
- the amount of any variable deductions: for example, tax, national insurance
- the net amount of the wages or salary
- the amount and method of each part-payment, when different parts of the net amount are paid in different ways: for instance, salary paid partly in cash and partly credited to a bank account.

Remuneration must be in 'the current coin of the realm' which includes bank notes. Payment by cheque, postal order or even into a bank account is, strictly speaking, not allowed unless mutually agreed between employee and employer.

The main items of deductions made from your gross salary are income tax and national insurance contributions.

income tax

You are taxed on your income in the 12-month period from 6 April one year to 5 April the next. There are allowances which will reduce the income on which you have to pay tax. For the 1981/82 tax year, these personal allowances are: single man or woman £1375, married man £2145; wife's earned income up to £1375. There are other allowances in addition – for instance, if supporting a dependent relative or if a single parent. And there is tax relief – for instance, on the interest on a mortgage loan.

After the various allowances and reliefs have been deducted, you pay (1981/82 tax year) 30 per cent tax on the first £11,250 of taxable income, 40 per cent on the next £2000, and then progessively higher rates in steps, up to 60 per cent on taxable income above £27,750.

Under the PAYE (pay-as-you-earn) scheme, employers must deduct from employees' pay the amount of income tax each employee is liable for according to his or her tax code, which is based on the allowable deductions. The employee thus gets his pay net of tax: the pay slip shows how much tax has been deducted.

Employers administer the PAYE scheme for all employees earning over £26·50 a week, £114·50 a month. The relevant amount of tax deducted from each payment you receive is based on your tax code – the higher the code number, the less tax you pay. The calculations ensure that 1/12th of your annual allowances is deducted each month if you are paid monthly (or 1/52nd each week if you are paid weekly) and that the due tax is taken from the rest. As an example, if your PAYE code is 207H, this means that you are entitled to £2079 of pay free of tax in the tax year. Tax tables provided by the Inland Revenue tell your employer that £173.25 a month or £40 a week of your income is non-taxable. A second set of tax tables tells him how much tax to deduct from the rest of your pay.

If either the amounts of allowances or rates of tax are changed, the Inland Revenue will send your employer a new set of tax tables based on the new rates. If your own circumstances change during the year, you should tell the Inland Revenue. Notice of coding, form P2, showing the allowances on which the code number is based is sent to you by the inspector of taxes, and if you do not agree with anything stated on that form, you should tell the tax office immediately. At the end of each tax year, the employer should give you a form P60, which is a certificate of gross earnings for the year and of income tax deducted under the PAYE scheme.

When you left your previous employment, your former employer should have completed for you the tripartite form P45. This shows your name, district tax office, code number, the week or month number of the last entry on your tax deduction card, total gross pay and total tax paid to date. If you did not get your P45, write to your previous employer and ask for it. He has to sent part 1 of this form to the inspector of taxes and to give you parts 2 and 3. It is important that you give these to your new employer, who should then send part 3 to the inspector of taxes.

Until the Inland Revenue confirms your tax code, your new employer will deduct tax on an emergency PAYE code – which assumes that you are a single person, without other allowances or deductions. When you get your correct code, you will get a refund of any tax that was over-deducted on the emergency code.

what you pay tax on

Income is widely defined. It includes salary, fees, wages, 'perquisites and profits'. You are taxed on, for example, overtime pay, commission, bonuses, fringe benefits such as gifts, tips, and goods supplied free, but not on expenses.

expenses

You do not normally have to pay tax on money your employer pays you to cover expenses to do with your job provided the money was spent 'wholly, exclusively and necessarily' in the performance of the duties of your employment. This is construed strictly: for example, if you live a long way from your normal place of work and have to stay in a hotel whenever you have to work late, you cannot claim the hotel costs as an allowable expense if your job could be done by another employee who does not live so far away. A sharp distinction is made between expenditure in the performance of the duties of employment (allowable as expenses) and expenditure incurred in order either to enable you to do the job initially – for instance, travelling expenses to get work – or to enable you to perform the duties of that office more efficiently – for instance, a training course paid for by yourself (neither allowable as expenses). You can, however, usually claim as expenses, special clothing and tools, and travelling in the course of employment.

There may be a settled practice in your company, agreed with the Inland Revenue, as to which expenses are allowable: check with your employer what, if any, such dispensations he has.

fringe benefits

Different rules apply to the taxing of fringe benefits if you are classed as a higher-paid earner: that is, if your earnings including all expenses, payments and benefits, are at the rate of £8500 a year or more, or if you are a company director (whatever your earnings). Then you get fewer 'perks' tax free and are normally taxed on the value of the fringe benefits – that is, the cost to the employer at the time of your getting them. (You have to give details to the Inland Revenue with your tax return; the employer has to give the information, too.)

For people not in the higher-paid category, the calculation is made on a more favourable basis and tax is payable only on those benefits which can be turned into cash by selling them. For example, if you were given a suit by your employer, tax is based on the full cost to the employer if you are classed as a higher-paid employee; otherwise, you are taxed on the estimated secondhand value – which would be much less.

Complex rules concern the tax treatment of a car as a fringe benefit. If a car is provided and paid for by your employer and you are a higher paid employee, your benefit from the private use of the car will be taxed according to set scales. The scales are based on the market value of the car when new, its age at the end of the tax year, its engine capacity. The mileage you drive for business and privately affects the multiple of the scale that you pay tax on. If the business element in your mileage is insubstantial – that is, under 2500 miles – the multiple is 1½ times; for business use between 2500 and 18,000 miles, the scale multiple is 1; if the business use is substantial (over 18,000 miles), the scale multiple is reduced to ½. In other words, the more business mileage, the less tax is payable. Driving to and from your normal place of work does not count as business mileage.

If you have the use of a car from an employer's car pool and do not take it home overnight, you will not normally be taxed on it at all, so long as any private use is merely incidental to business use.

If you are a higher-paid employee and you (or a relative of yours) have a loan from the employer either interest-free or at a lower rate than the official rate (at present, 15 per cent), the saving on the interest you pay is taxable once the value of the saving comes to over £200. This does not apply to interest on a loan which qualifies for tax relief – or would qualify if interest were paid – such as a loan for house purchase.

Where the employer pays the premiums for a private medical insurance scheme, these count as a taxable benefit if you are a higher-paid employee.

Whether you are a higher-paid employee or not, if your employer places goods at your disposal (for example, a television set), you pay tax on 20 per cent of its market value when you first get it. You pay tax also on vouchers or tokens which can be exchanged for goods or services, based on the amount the employer pays out.

You will, in general, be taxed on living accommodation provided free or at a low rent as part of your employment. The amount taxed is either the rental value of the property in the open market or the actual rent paid by your employer, whichever is the greater. You are exempted, however, if you have to live in the accommodation in order to perform your duties properly (for example, a house-master at a public school); if it is customary to your type of employment to have such accommodation provided (for example, a policeman) or if your employment involves you in a security risk (for example, the prime minister).

The *Money Which? Tax-Saving Guide* published in March each year includes more information about tax and fringe benefits. The Inland Revenue booklet (no 480) provides detailed *Notes on expenses, payments and benefits for directors and certain employees*, and is available free from tax offices.

national insurance contributions

National insurance contributions must be paid by all employed earners, with the following exceptions:

- if you are below the age of 16
- if you have reached pensionable age (women 60, men 65)
- if you are paid less than the 'lower earnings limit': for the 1981/82 tax year, £27 per week (£117 per month, £1404 per year)
- if you are not resident in the UK.

You pay class 1 contributions if you work under a contract of employment or apprenticeship, or hold an office and pay income tax under schedule E.

You pay a percentage of your total earnings up to the upper earnings limit. For the 1981/82 tax year, the upper earnings limit is £200 per week, £10,400 per year. The standard rate percentage is 7.75 per cent on the whole amount up to £200 per week. For people contracted-out of the state additional pension scheme, it is lower: 7.75 per cent on the first £27 per week and 5.25 per cent on the slice between £27 and £200. Your employer pays a contribution of nearly twice yours. Married women and widows who chose to pay contributions at a reduced rate pay 2 per cent of their earnings (this choice is no longer available).

Every employed person has a national insurance number which goes with him or her throughout their working lives. It appears on the payslip (and on other forms such as the P45 on changing jobs). National insurance contributions made (or credited) are recorded against this number, and it has to be quoted when you claim any 'benefit'.

By paying class 1 contributions regularly, you become eligible to claim a benefit when you are

- unemployed
- sick
- pregnant
- retired
- disabled
- widowed

In order to be eligible for some benefits, it is necessary to have made or been credited with a certain minimum number of contributions.

in the job

On changing jobs, it is well to ask yourself whether the extent of non-work activity is different from that in your previous job, and whether it will affect you in any way, beneficially or otherwise.

union membership

Your privileges and obligations in your trade union are governed by the contract of membership. Its terms are in the union rule books and implied by custom and practice. The rights include

- the right to resign from the union on reasonable notice and subject to reasonable conditions (for example, after you have paid any arrears of subscription)
- the right to refuse to contribute to the union's political fund
- the rules of natural justice as laid down at common law (for instance, if there is any question of union disciplinary action for, say, refusing to participate in a strike, you must have full notice of the charges against you, and the opportunity to state your case before an unbiased disciplinary committee)
- no discrimination on an application to join, or against an existing member, on the grounds of sex, race or EEC nationality.

It is unfair to dismiss an employee for exercising his or her rights of trade union membership and activities. This protection exists without any qualifying weeks of employment, and covers part-time employees, too.

To be valid, the activities you take part in must be 'of' your trade union – this does not mean your own campaigning activities without official trade union approval. Activities that are normally protected include recruiting members, collecting subscriptions, distributing literature for the union. Such activities must be reasonable and not cause substantial inconvenience to your employer. An 'appropriate' time for trade union activities is defined as outside working hours or during working hours with your employer's consent.

You can complain to an industrial tribunal if action short of dismissal were taken to prevent or deter you from exercising your trade union rights or if you were penalised for so doing. Such action might take the form of not being granted voluntary overtime or a Christmas bonus, or an unjustified refusal of promotion.

Employment protection does not extend to an applicant being not appointed because of his or her past trade union activities: firms may maintain black lists with impunity.

closed shop

A union closed shop takes many different forms, from the strict pre-entry closed shop where you need a union card even to apply for a job, as in printing and the theatre, to the very loose arrangements which have grown up as custom and practice and may not be at all strictly enforced. A closed shop is broadly defined as 'any agreement or arrangement, whether or not in writing, entered into by an independent recognised union which has the effect of requiring employees of a particular class to join a specified union or unions'.

Members of a union not specified in the agreement, or employees who refuse to join a union at all, may be dismissed or may have action short of dismissal taken against them without redress unless

- they object to joining the union on religious grounds or because of conscience or other deeply held personal convictions, or
- they have not been union members prior to and since the closed shop was established, or
- the closed shop came into operation after 15 August 1980 and was not approved by at least 80 per cent of the employees entitled to vote in a secret ballot, or
- the union specified in the agreement is not independent.

An 'independent' trade union is one which is not under the domination of an employer and not liable to interference tending towards an employer's control through financial or material support. Single company in-house staff associations are most at risk of being dependent. A certificate of independence given by the certification officer of trade unions and employers' associations is conclusive; all TUC-affiliated unions have such an endorsement.

Anyone working where a closed shop exists who is excluded or unreasonably expelled from the union may complain to an industrial tribunal. If, as a result, the applicant is admitted or re-admitted to membership of the union, he may make an application for compensation for any loss sustained.

The TUC (Congress House, Great Russell Street, London WC1B 3LS) has established an independent review committee to hear complaints of exclusion or expulsion from member unions. It would seem sensible for anyone excluded or expelled from a union to make use of the TUC machinery in addition to or instead of lodging a complaint to an industrial tribunal.

The TUC has published a *Handbook on the Employment Act 1980* (price 75p). Booklet no 7 in the Department of Employment's employment protection series deals with *Union membership rights and the closed shop*.

discrimination

The Race Relations Act, the Equal Pay Act and the Sex Discrimination Act give a right of action if you are discriminated against in employment (also education, housing or the provision of goods, facilities and services) on the grounds of

- race, colour, nationality, ethnic or national origins
- sex
- being married.

Religion is not specifically covered except in Northern Ireland under the Fair Employment Act.

The Race Relations Act and Sex Discrimination Act outlaw all forms of discrimination: direct, indirect, racial segregation, victimisation, pressurising—and retaliation has been added by court decision.

– *direct discrimination* arises where a person treats you less favourably than others are treated or would be treated in the same circumstances: for instance, segregating a person constitutes less favourable treatment.

– *indirect discrimination* covers practices which, while not necessarily discriminatory in intention, are discriminatory in effect. It arises when someone applies to you a requirement or condition which, even though it applies equally to all other persons, is such that the proportion of people of your race or sex who can comply with it is considerably smaller than the proportion of people outside your race or sex who can comply with it; is not justifiable on other grounds; is to your detriment because you cannot comply with it.

The justifiability of a condition or requirement depends on whether the condition is genuine and necessary, not merely convenient; whether its discriminatory effect is balanced by the need for it; whether the employer could achieve the objectives he sets by some other non-discriminatory method. For instance, in one case the employer's requirement for "no floppy long hair, or beard" in a chocolate factory was held to be justified on the grounds of health and safety.

If you come across a discriminatory condition, even if you can comply with it so that there is no detriment to you personally, you can complain to the Equal Opportunities Commission or the Commission for Racial Equality. They can institute a formal investigation and, if they make a finding of such a practice, can issue a non-discrimination notice to restrain the employer from the discriminatory practice. If this does not bring it to an end, the Commission may apply to a county court for an injunction.

– *victimisation* can be claimed if you are treated less favourably by your employer (or prospective employer) because you complained of discrimination against you or someone else or because of your involvement in a complaint of discrimination, initiated either by you or by someone else.

It is unlawful to aid an act of discrimination committed by another person. An employer is liable for discrimination carried out by his employees in the course of employment unless he can prove that he took all reasonably practicable steps to prevent the employees from doing that act. It is unlawful for a person to instruct or to pressurise another person to discriminate.

Being dismissed as retaliation for refusing to obey an order to discriminate has been held to be unfair dismissal.

The context of possible discrimination in employment is very wide. It specifically includes discrimination arising in connection with

- arrangements for recruitment: you can claim if you are put off applying for a job. It is no defence that the prospective employer wanted to keep a balance between the sexes or races. Discriminatory advertisements can be restrained by the intervention of the Equal Opportunities Commission or the Commission for Racial Equality. The use of words with a gender connotation, such as 'sales girl' or 'waitress' is taken to indicate an intention to discriminate.
- refusal to make an offer of employment
- different terms and conditions of employment
- application for transfer or promotion
- selection for training (an employer can, however, take positive steps to train a minority group if the racial or sexual group favoured has been under-represented in his company during any time in the previous 12 months)
- allocation of any fringe benefits, such as loans, medical care, cars, bonuses or travel
- dismissal.

permissible discrimination

There are certain exceptions to both the race and sex discrimination legislation. Where being of one sex or race is a genuine occupational qualification, you may justifiably be refused a position if you are of the other.

An employer is allowed to discriminate on the grounds of sex if he can prove that the essential nature of the job calls for a man because of his physiology (for example, a model) but not for his greater strength and stamina. A man may be required for authenticity in entertainment (a casting director, for instance, need not interview women for the part of King Lear). Decency or privacy may require the job to be done by only men or only women.

Accommodation may be a factor where the employee is required to live on the job and the employer cannot reasonably provide separate sleeping and sanitary facilities (for example, seamen); or the job is at a single sex establishment where people require supervision (for example, a prison officer) or the job is one of two which are to be held by a married couple.

The Sex Discrimination Act does not apply to provisions in relation to retirement (but there must be equal access to occupational pension schemes), nor to undertakings with less than 5 employees. Special treatment afforded to employed women in connection with pregnancy or childbirth also does not count as discrimination.

An employer is allowed to discriminate on the grounds of race in some narrower circumstances – for instance, where a member of a particular race is required for reasons of authenticity in art or photography or in a bar or restaurant with a particular ambiance (such as a waiter in a chinese restaurant).

Discriminatory acts to safeguard national security are excluded from the legislation; private households also are outside the legislation.

making a claim

You can make a claim for discrimination in employment not only against an employer but also against a trade union or employers' organisation; an employment agency; the Manpower Services Commission. A claim has to be made to an industrial tribunal within three months of the discriminatory happening.

You can get advice about the grounds for a claim, about sex discrimination and rights to equal pay from the Equal Opportunities Commission, Overseas House, Quay Street, Manchester M3 3HN (in

Scotland, 249 West George Street, Glasgow G2 4QE; in Wales, Caerwys House, Windsor Place, Cardiff CF1 1LB; in Northern Ireland, Lindsay House, Callender Street, Belfast BT1 5DT).

Advice about cases of race discrimination is available from the Commission for Racial Equality, Elliot House, 10–12 Arlington Street, London SW1E 5EH.

Both organisations publish leaflets and guides about the scope and interpretation of the respective acts and the roles of the two Commissions. The Home Office has published guides to the Sex Discrimination Act and to the Race Relations Act; these are available free from the Home Office library, 50 Queen Anne's Gate, London SW1H 9AT.

Both the Equal Opportunities Commission and the Commission for Racial Equality may arrange legal representation, particularly if your case raises matters of principle or is specially complex. The Equal Opportunities Commission has published a clear and detailed guide on *How to prepare your own case for an industrial tribunal*, including specimen forms, for claims under the Sex Discrimination Act and the Equal Pay Act.

There is a special questionnaire form to send to the employer about the reasons for his actions (the Commission for Racial Equality or the Equal Opportunities Commission can supply you with the appropriate form). The employer is not legally bound to answer but, if he does not, or replies in an evasive or equivocal manner, the industrial tribunal may draw its own conclusions from this.

At a hearing, the onus of proof is on you – and discrimination is one of the most difficult matters to prove. You must be well prepared with witnesses and documentary evidence. It is easy for an employer to put forward alternative reasons for his actions, and you may have to rely on inferences of discrimination.

The remedies available at the industrial tribunal are

- a declaration that you have been discriminated against
- a recommendation that the employer (or other respondent) take a particular course of action in order to reduce the adverse effect of the act of discrimination
- compensation: you can be compensated for loss of earnings, future prospects, and a small amount for injury to feelings – up to a maximum of £6250 in all.

spent convictions

Under the Rehabilitation of Offenders Act, after a certain period of time an ex-criminal's conviction becomes 'spent'. An employer must not disclose it in a reference, and it is not a proper ground for dismissal or discrimination in any way.

An offence becomes spent according to the sentence:

imprisonment over 30 months	never spent
imprisonment between 6 and 30 months	after 10 years
imprisonment less than 6 months	after 7 years
fine or community service order	after 5 years
conditional discharge or probation	after 1 year

There are, however, exceptions for certain jobs and professions in which offences can never become spent. The list includes doctors, dentists, lawyers, accountants, veterinary surgeons, teachers.

maternity

A pregnant employee can claim from her employer

- the right not to be dismissed for reasons connected with the pregnancy
- the right to have time off for antenatal care
- the right to maternity pay from her employer
- the right to return to work after the confinement.

There is a Department of Employment leaflet (no 4 in the employment protection series) on *Employment rights for the expectant mother*. Any contractual provisions made by an individual employer which are more favourable than the statutory rights will take precedence.

If the requisite national insurance contributions have been paid or credited, a woman who is pregnant can claim maternity benefits from the state: a maternity grant, which is a lump sum, and a maternity allowance which is paid for 18 weeks – from 11 weeks before the expected date of birth up to the end of the sixth week after the confinement. DHSS leaflet NI 17A gives details of the conditions for claiming these benefits.

dismissal

A dismissal connected with pregnancy is normally automatically unfair. This covers, for example, being sacked because of the amount of sick leave you take or because you take too much time off to attend antenatal classes. To be able to claim this right, you must have been working for the same employer for 52 weeks for at least 16 hours a week (or more than 8 hours a week for 5 years or more). The exception is that if on or after 1 October 1980 you joined a firm employing fewer than 21 employees, the qualifying period of work is 104 weeks with the employer so long as the number of people he employs never exceeds 20.

Dismissal is not unfair, however, if you can no longer adequately do your work or if continuing to work would be breaking some other law – for example, about health and safety at work. In such a case, the employer must offer a suitable alternative job, if one exists, on terms not substantially less favourable than the current post, and is justified in dismissing you if you unreasonably refuse this.

maternity pay

You are entitled to payment from your employer for up to 6 weeks while off work for pregnancy or confinement. The employer must give you 90 per cent of your normal week's pay in a lump sum or in weekly or monthly instalments, but can deduct from this the state maternity allowance (whether you qualify for it or not), any payment you are entitled to under your contract, national insurance contributions and tax. (He, in turn, can reclaim the money from the maternity pay fund financed by employers' national insurance contributions.)

You are entitled to maternity pay whether or not you intend to return to work after your pregnancy, provided that

- you have been employed until at least the 11th week before your expected week of confinement (the week for these purposes begins on sunday morning)
- before that 11th week, you have been continuously employed by your employer or an associated employer for at least 104 weeks
- you inform your employer in writing, 21 days before your absence begins or as soon as is reasonably practicable.

You must, if requested, produce a doctor's or midwife's certificate stating the expected week of confinement.

antenatal care

All women have the right not to be unreasonably refused time off for antenatal care, and to be paid for that time off. If asked to do so, the woman must produce proof, such as an appointment card. The appointments must be authorised by a doctor, midwife, or health visitor.

maternity leave

For the right to maternity leave, you must have worked for the same employer for at least 16 hours a week for two years or more as at the 11th week before the expected date of confinement (or for less than 16 hours but more than 8 hours a week, for 5 years or more).

You can leave 11 weeks before the expected date of the birth and stay away up to 29 weeks after the birth. You do not get your salary or wages during maternity leave. But you do not have to leave at the 11th week and may continue working for as long as you are able to do so. Similarly, you may return to work before the end of the 29-week period.

You have a right to return to the same job at any time before the end of the period of 29 weeks beginning with the week in which your baby is born. On your return, your terms of pay, seniority, pension rights must be not less favourable than before your pregnancy. Moreover, if there has been a pay rise in your absence, you are entitled to the new rate, and your period of employment is treated as continuous.

A woman who works for an employer with fewer than 6 employees at the time she goes on maternity leave is not automatically entitled to the same job back.

There are other conditions to be observed in exercising this right:

- at least 21 days before your absence or as soon as is reasonably practicable, you must inform your employer in writing that you intend to return to work, and inform him of the expected week of confinement
- if so requested by your employer any time after 49 days after the birth, you must give written confirmation that you do intend to return to work; your reply should be within 14 days of his letter (or as soon as is reasonably practicable thereafter)
- you must give written notice 21 days in advance of your return.

You can extend your absence for up to 4 weeks if you produce a medical certificate stating that you are unfit to return to work. On the other hand, your employer can postpone your return for up to 4 weeks if he gives a reason for doing so.

An employer not allowing you to return to your old job after maternity counts as unfair dismissal. Only when it is not reasonably practicable for the employer to take a woman back in her old job, or to offer her suitable alternative work, will failure to permit her to return not be treated as unfair dismissal.

illness

There is no statutory or common law right to be paid during sickness. This is a matter for negotiation with the employer either individually or, more commonly, through a trade union. In practice, many employees receive wages during sickness under a sick pay scheme operated by their employer.

Irrespective of any arrangements an employer may have for staff who are ill, anyone who is incapable of work because of illness or disablement, can claim sickness benefit from the state if he or she has paid the requisite number of national insurance contributions. (Details are given in the DHSS leaflet NI 16, available at social security offices.)

To claim, you have to have a statement from a doctor (medical certificate, a note or a form) and send this to the social security office within 6 days (or 21 days if it is the first time you have ever claimed). You have to give your national insurance number and indicate whether you wish to claim for dependants.

If your doctor gives you a 'closed' sick note, this will have the date on which he considers you can return to work. If it is an 'open' note, you will have to go back to the doctor when it expires to get a date for your return to work or another 'open' note if he considers you are still unfit. Every time you get a note from the doctor, you should send this to the social security office so that your sickness benefit continues.

You will get payment for six days (not sundays) each week you are sick, consisting of the basic benefit (currently £20.65 a week or one-sixth of that per odd day, going up to £22.50 in November 1981) plus extra for each dependant (currently £12.75 a week for an adult, £1.25 for a child). For periods of illness starting before 2 January 1982, you will also get an earnings-related supplement (maximum £14) if you had paid sufficient class 1 national insurance contributions in the 1979/80 tax year. The total you can be paid in all is 85 per cent of your weekly earnings on which your entitlement to the supplement is based (now £135 a week).

Sickness benefit is not taxable (yet) and you are credited with national insurance contributions while you are receiving it.

You will be disqualified from benefit for up to 6 weeks if the incapacity arose as a result of your misconduct (for example, voluntary alcoholism). You will also be disqualified if you fail without good cause to attend or submit to medical or other examination or treatment which is reasonable in the circumstances, or if you behave in a way calculated to retard your recovery. You can appeal against a decision to withhold sickness benefit by applying to the medical appeal tribunal, which is chaired by a doctor, with two lay members.

If you do some work while you are off sick you should tell the DHSS office, and if you earn more than £15 a week (after deducting allowable expenses), your sickness benefit will be stopped.

However, if your employer continues to pay your salary while you are sick, this does not affect your receiving sickness benefit as well. Your employer may, however, stipulate that you hand over to him any sickness benefit that you get. And if you qualify for any other national insurance benefit (for example, widow's benefit or maternity allowance), you cannot be paid both but will normally get an amount equal to the higher benefit.

The maximum period for which sickness benefit will be paid is 168 days (28 weeks excluding sundays). The 168 days do not have to be in a continuous period: separate spells of sickness of four days or more can be added together and treated as one period of interruption of work provided there is not more than 8 weeks between each spell.

If you are still not capable of work at the end of that period, you are then automatically switched to invalidity benefit. (DHSS leaflet NI 16A describes this.) Invalidity benefit is paid for as long as you continue to be incapable of work, provided you produce a doctor's statement at regular intervals to substantiate your incapacity.

Someone who has not qualified for sickness benefit but who has been off work sick for 28 weeks or more can then claim a non-contributory invalidity pension which does not depend on how many national insurance contributions have been paid. (DHSS leaflet NI 210 gives details.)

long illness

Many companies continue to pay employees' full salaries during a number of weeks' illness (13, say) and half-pay for a further period (another 13 weeks, say). Alternatively, a company may top up any state sickness benefit to a specified level that relates to salary.

When you are on reduced pay, the company may pay your as well as their own contributions to the pension scheme. These contributions may relate to your reduced salary rather than your full salary (this could affect your final pension entitlement).

The company is unlikely to continue to pay you, even at a reduced rate, for an indefinite period if you continue to be ill. The firm may, however, have a group permanent health or salary-continuation-during-illness insurance policy, which would provide a payment equivalent to a reduced salary, probably until the retirement age for that employment. Such a policy may or may not provide pension contributions as part of the benefits. If it does not, ask whether the employer will pay them. A report on *Permanent health insurance* was published in *Money Which?* June 1980.

In the case of prolonged ill health or incapacity, it is often possible to retire early from a pension scheme. The scheme rules may allow a better pension than for someone who retires early in good health. For example, instead of counting only the number of years of membership in the scheme, many schemes count the prospective number of years to normal retirement age. Also, any rule about normal minimum retirement age is usually waived. Even so, a salary-continuation insurance scheme may be financially better for you than getting an early pension.

industrial disease

Someone whose illness is recognised as a 'prescribed' industrial disease is entitled to industrial injury benefit without any national insurance contribution conditions being applied. This benefit is at a higher rate than sickness benefit. However, not all prescribed diseases qualify for payment of injury benefit. After the end of the injury benefit period, or if not entitled to injury benefit, you may be entitled to disablement benefit. This takes the form of a weekly pension if your disability is assessed at over 20 per cent, usually a lump sum if under that extent.

The prescribed diseases are specified in DHSS leaflet NI 2. They include poisoning by a number of specific noxious substances in an occupation involving the use and handling of or exposure to the fumes, dust or vapour of the substances. Also qualifying is the effect on various parts of the body of specific manual labour, such as prolonged periods of repetitive movements. Certain skin and lung diseases and cancers are on the list. There are at present over 50 prescribed diseases, and others may be added from time to time.

To claim benefit, the disease must have arisen due to the nature of your work and you must be employed in an occupation recognised by the government as giving rise to the risk of that disease. There is a special rate of disablement benefit for pneumoconiosis and similar lung diseases (DHSS leaflet NI 3 explains) and there are special qualifying conditions for claiming benefit for occupational deafness (see DHSS leaflet NI 207).

accident at work

If you are injured as a result of an accident at work and are unable to work, you can claim industrial injury benefit irrespective of national insurance contributions. DHSS leaflet NI 5 explains the circumstances for claiming injury benefit because of an accident at work.

An accident, for industrial injury benefit purposes, means any unexpected happening or incident arising out of and in the course of your work resulting in personal injury. It does not matter whether the effect of the injury is immediate (for example, if you break a leg in a fall) or delayed (for example, if a minor cut later turns septic).

Generally, an accident which happens when you are at work is treated as having occurred as a result of your work unless there is evidence to the contrary. Whether or not you are considered to be at work at a particular time depends on the circumstances. For instance, you are not normally regarded as being at work when travelling to or from work.

If you have an accident at work, you should tell your employer or foreman or someone in authority at once. If you cannot do it yourself, get someone to do it for you. It is important that you should report the accident as soon as possible after it happens, otherwise you might have difficulty in proving your claim. If there is an accident book, you or someone on your behalf should enter details of the accident in it as soon as possible after the accident.

If there is no means of recording the accident, send a note or a letter to your employer giving your name and address, age and sex, occupation, the cause and nature of the injury, and the date, place and circumstances of the accident. If someone else notifies the accident for you, he or she should give his or her name, address and occupation.

Even if the accident does not seem serious at the time, make sure that it is reported to your employer while the facts are fresh in people's minds, in case later on you suffer incapacity or disablement as a result of the accident.

A member of a trade union should seek the advice of the union – this is an area in which the union can be of great help to individual members.

Industrial injury benefit is £2.75 a week more than sickness benefit. It is paid for up to 6 months after an accident as long as you remain incapable of work because of the accident.

Following assessment by a medical board, you may become eligible for disablement benefit, either a lump sum or a weekly pension, depending on the degree of disablement. You may possibly be eligible for extra allowances. For instance, someone likely to be permanently unable to work may get an unemployability supplement added to a disablement pension.

Another extra allowance is hardship allowance. You may be entitled to this, if, because of the effects of disablement due to the accident, you are unable to return to your regular occupation or to do work of an equivalent standard. The rate of the allowance will be, broadly, the difference (subject to a specified maximum) between the current level of earnings in your former regular occupation and that in any alternative occupation which you are capable of following.

DHSS leaflet NI 6 gives details of disablement benefit and increases, and a claim form (BI 100A) is available at social security offices.

Quite apart from statutory provision, you may have a claim for damages against your employer in negligence. The law requires all employers to have insurance for liability for personal injury to their employees.

suspension on medical grounds

Some jobs are covered by special health and safety regulations under which an employer may suspend an employee from normal work because the employee's health would be endangered if he or she continued to be exposed to the particular substance – for example, when working with ionising radiation, lead and certain chemicals. When an adviser from the Employment Medical Advisory Service informs the employer of the danger to the employees, they must then be suspended until the doctor says that it is safe to start work again.

Employees who are so suspended have a right to payment of a normal week's pay for up to 26 weeks. The amount is calculated in accordance with the normal rules. But employees will not get medical suspension pay if

- they have not been employed continuously for four weeks before suspension begins
- at any time they are not able to work because they are ill or physically or mentally disabled (during which time they get other state benefits)
- they unreasonably refuse to do suitable alternative work that their employer offers
- they do not meet any reasonable requirements their employer may impose.

If the job of an employee suspended on medical grounds is taken over by another worker hired specifically for this purpose, the substitute can be dismissed when the original employee returns, provided the substitute was informed, in writing, at the time he or she was taken on that this would happen. The Department of Employment booklet no 5 in the employment protection series deals with *Suspension on medical grounds under health and safety regulations*.

health and safety at work

Before 1974, there was a hotch-potch of some 31 statutes, such as the Factories Act and the Office, Shops and Railways Premises Act, and some 500 regulations covering the field of safety at work. The aim of the Health and Safety at Work Act 1974 was to provide a comprehensive and integrated system of law to deal with the health and safety of virtually all people at work and the risks to others arising from work activities. This is ultimately to be achieved by regulations and codes of practice. Some of these have been introduced to amplify and extend the duties of the 1974 Act, but many of the earlier requirements of the older legislation remain in force.

The main duty lies on the employer to ensure, so far as is reasonably practicable, the health and safety and welfare at work of all his employees. This applies in particular to the provision of safe plant, and the maintenance of all machinery, equipment and appliances used – and covers all work places including offices and shops as well as factories.

Welfare includes room temperature, ventilation, lighting, provision of lavatories, washbasins and drinking water, seating, first aid arrangements.

The Fire Precautions Act requires premises to be provided with reasonable means of escape and certain fire-fighting equipment. Larger premises must have a fire certificate issued by the local fire authority. A fire certificate requires the provision and maintenance of means of escape, means for fighting fire and means for giving people on the premises warning in case of fire. It also requires staff to be instructed and trained in what to do in the event of an emergency, and regular fire drills for the staff to be held.

There is an implied term in all contracts of employment that the employer will take reasonable care of your safety. This means providing

- safe working practices whether by supervision, disciplinary procedures or safety equipment
- safe tools, equipment and materials
- trained and efficient personnel.

Your employer is liable for all reasonably foreseeable consequences of failure to take such reasonable care, and employer's liability insurance is compulsory.

For your part, as an employee, you must take reasonable care for your own safety and that of others, and cooperate with your employer in arrangements to meet the basic safety standards.

An employer must provide his employees with all necessary information and training in safe practices. If he employs 5 or more people, he must prepare a written statement of his general policy, organisation and arrangements for health and safety at work, keep it up to date and bring it to the notice of all employees.

Employers who negotiate with independent trade unions must allow them to appoint safety representatives from among the workforce and consult them on health and safety arrangements. The representatives should have been employed by the employer throughout the preceding two years or have had at least two years' experience in similar employment. They represent employees in consultations over health and safety arrangements, and investigate potential hazards and complaints. At the request of at least two safety representatives, the employer must establish a safety committee.

Employers must allow the safety representatives time off with pay to train for and perform these functions; if the employer fails to do so, the representatives may make a complaint to an industrial tribunal.

If there is no safety representation at your place of work, ask your employer to set it up.

enforcement

Enforcement is generally carried out by health and safety inspectors from the Health and Safety Executive; for most shop and office activities, enforcement is by inspectors appointed by the local authority.

Any employee can report any circumstances which appear to contravene the requirements for safety conditions at work to the local area office of the Health and Safety Executive (listed in telephone directories) or to the Executive's headquarters at Baynards House, 1 Chepstow Place, London W2 4TF (or to the local authority if appropriate). The Executive issues free explanatory leaflets including advice to employees and employers.

An inspector will normally give oral or written advice to the employer and to employees' representatives about any matter of health or safety at work which requires attention. In addition, he can

- issue an improvement notice requiring that the fault be remedied within a specific time
- issue a prohibition notice if there is a risk of serious personal injury, stopping the activity giving rise to this risk until the remedial action specified in the notice has been taken (and if a person on whom an improvement or prohibition notice is served fails to comply with it, he is liable to prosecution)
- seize, render harmless, or destroy any substance or article he considers to be the cause of imminent danger or serious personal injury.

In addition, a health and safety inspector can prosecute any person contravening the legislation. Prosecution is usually in a magistrates court and carries a fine of up to £1000 (but if it gets to the crown court, there is no upper limit).

strikes

A strike, and probably also a work-to-rule or go-slow, is technically a breach of contract: your employer can, in theory, claim damages – but would have to take you to court for this. In practice, damages would be difficult to assess, and an employer is more likely simply to withhold pay for any day of strike.

Trade unions, as bodies, are immune from being sued for damages in relation to industrial action but individual trade union officers and members are only protected where their acts are 'in contemplation or furtherance of a trade dispute'. Trade dispute includes action related to terms and conditions of work; engagement of employees; allocation of work; matters of discipline; trade union membership; negotiating machinery. Most strikes come under the heading of trade dispute but political strikes do not, nor those concerned with personal grudges.

You cannot claim unemployment benefit for the days you are on strike, and you lose your right to guarantee payment for the period of the strike (if you become eligible, you can claim supplementary benefit – but only for dependants, and the amount will be reduced by

£12, the notional strike pay, whether your union provides it or not; DHSS leaflet SB2 gives details).

The time you are on strike does not break continuity of employment but you cannot count any week during which you were on strike towards the qualifying period. If, while you are on strike, you are dismissed together with all the others on strike and none of the people who participated in the strike is re-engaged, your dismissal will not be considered unfair.

discipline

The employer must make clear to all employees his disciplinary rules and procedure for dealing with grievances. The person to whom the employee can apply must be specified and also the manner in which an application should be made if the employee is dissatisfied with a disciplinary decision or wants to seek redress for any grievance. This information must be given either in the contract of employment or with the written statement an employee receives after 13 weeks of new employment.

Broadly, disciplinary procedures should be agreed between management and unions (or other employee representatives). There should be a clear and concise statement, in writing, of

- the range of disciplinary actions and who in management can take what particular disciplinary decisions
- the employee to whom they apply.

Disciplinary procedures should ensure that every case is carefully investigated and reasons given for any penalty. They should give the employee the right to be heard and to be accompanied by a trade union representative or fellow employee, and provide a right of appeal. Dismissal for a first breach should not be allowed except where the employee's misconduct is particularly gross.

It could be fair to dismiss without giving an employee the opportunity to explain if the employee has already clearly stated why he is adopting the attitude complained of; also where, whatever the explanation, an employee's continued employment would be injurious to the business.

sanctions

The disciplinary sanctions open to an employer for misconduct by an employee range from fines, withholding bonuses, denial of promotion, to suspension and dismissal. The legality or otherwise of any such measures is for most people governed by their contract of employment.

Fines, and deductions from pay, can be made only where permitted by your contract of employment or by well-established and recognised custom and practice. Otherwise, if your employer fines you or deducts pay, you may leave (without giving notice, if you wish) and claim to have been constructively dismissed by reason of the employer's conduct. Even where a penalty is written into the contract, a court would strike down any penalty that is more than a genuine estimate of the damages likely to result from your misconduct.

More specific conditions are laid down in the Truck Acts for manual workers. Under these old statutes, deductions from wages may be made only for 'bad or negligent work or injury to the materials or other property of the employer' and then only if

- you have signed a written contract
- you have been furnished with written particulars of the offences and amounts of fines or deductions, or you have access to a notice specifying deductions that is displayed in a prominent place
- the event causes loss or hindrance to your employer
- the amount fined or deducted is reasonable
- your employer keeps a register of all fines.

Your employer can suspend you on full pay (unless you belong to the restricted class of employees who have an implied right to be provided with work). He cannot, however, suspend you without pay unless there is a clause to that effect in your contract. If the contract provides for suspension without pay or with pay in certain circumstances, and your employer suspends you for other reasons, that is a breach of the contract.

Except in the most serious acts of misconduct, the employer should, before suspension or dismissal, give

- a formal oral warning
- or, for more serious issues, a written warning setting out the nature of the offence and the likely consequence of further offences, with a time limit
- a final written warning, also with a time limit.

Any disciplinary action should take into consideration the past record of the employee – that is, his length of service and quality of service – and any acts or omissions on the part of management.

The ACAS (Advisory Conciliation and Arbitration Service) code of practice no 1 *Disciplinary practice and procedures in employment* (15p from HMSO) gives guidelines for employers and employees.

breach of contract

Broadly, the consequences of a breach of contract by an employee are that

- he may be disciplined in accordance with contractual procedures
- the employer may sue for damages in the county court (sheriff court in Scotland) – but this is very rare
- the employer may apply for an injunction (interdict in Scotland) to prevent the employee's breach – this may happen where the employee is infringing a restrictive covenant or using trade secrets
- if the breach is very serious, the employer may summarily dismiss the employee.

If it is the employer who breaches the contract, the usual consequences are that the employee may

- claim wrongful dismissal in the county court (or sheriff court)
- claim unfair dismissal in an industrial tribunal
- sue the employer for damages in a county court (or sheriff court)
- leave and claim to have been constructively dismissed.

For instance, in cases of disciplinary suspension, demotion or transfer which are in breach of contract, you can leave and make a claim for constructive dismissal.

constructive dismissal

If your employer makes things so difficult for you that you resign in protest, this counts as 'constructive' dismissal. Your employer must have broken the contract in a fundamental respect or shown that he no longer intends to be bound by an essential term of it. It is difficult in any particular case to know whether there has been a constructive dismissal. You should, therefore, seek advice (from trade union, lawyer, CAB or advice centre) before taking any decisive steps. Examples of what have counted as constructive dismissal include demotion;

suspension without pay; a pay cut; unreasonable insistence on a change of place or hours of work; making life intolerable for the employee.

It is best to put in writing the circumstances of your employment and that your employer's breach in such-and-such a respect is the reason why you are leaving. And you should leave as soon after the breach as possible – the longer you stay at work, the less likely an industrial tribunal is to infer that you left in consequence of your employer's actions.

Gone

Dismissal

The ultimate disciplinary sanction is dismissal, but there is only a limited set of circumstances when dismissal is not unfair. These include

- your lack of capability or qualification for performing work of the kind you were employed to do (this includes skill, aptitude, health, physical or mental qualities)
- your misconduct.

lack of capability

If your employer considers your work performance inadequate he should show

- what was required of you and that this was reasonable
- that you were informed of or must have been aware of these requirements
- that you fell short of them.

He should in most cases give written warnings, and an opportunity to improve, unless this would obviously be fruitless.

The majority of cases is concerned with ill health. Broadly, your employer should consult you and discuss your health problems with you and get a fully informed picture, including medical reports, of your problem. An employer does not have access to an employee's medical records without the employee's consent but he may ask him or her to agree to a medical examination or to make available a report from the employee's own doctor.

The employer should consider whether he can make any alternative work available for you during your incapacity, but does not have to create a new job for you.

misconduct

The amorphous category of misconduct includes continued wilful disobedience, frequent rudeness and aggressiveness, persistent absenteeism and lateness, bad timekeeping. If your employer has tacitly accepted or condoned a particular breach of rules in the past, he may have to show why this breach was so bad as to justify dismissal.

Disobedience to rules also counts as misconduct. The rules should have been brought to your notice, and be reasonable and lawful.

Gross misconduct includes a criminal offence committed while in your job, or which may affect your job. Most commonly, this would be theft, fraud, violence or industrial espionage. It does not refer to a crime committed outside your hours of employment unless it renders you unsuitable in some way for your work. Your employer must reasonably believe that you have committed the offence when he dismisses you (not sacking you and then later finding out about various misdemeanours). As long as he thinks on reasonable grounds that you have offended, it does not render the dismissal unfair if it is subsequently established in a criminal court that no offence was committed, or that it was committed by someone else.

In most cases, your employer should give you a reasonable chance to explain your side of the story.

other reasons for dismissal

A replacement employee where the regular employee was temporarily absent due to medical suspension or pregnancy can be dismissed provided that the replacement was warned of the temporary nature of his or her employment at the time of engagement.

Where an employer could not continue to employ the individual without contravening an act of parliament, he can dismiss the employee. For example, a lorry driver who loses his driving licence cannot continue to be employed as a driver and the employer is not under a duty to offer him alternative employment.

receiving notice

If your employer wants to bring your contract to an end, he must give you at least the notice laid down in the Employment Protection (Consolidation) Act or the notice required by your contract of service, whichever is most favourable to you.

This does not apply if

- you agree to accept shorter notice, or
- your conduct entitles your employer to terminate your employment without notice, or
- your contract was for a fixed term.

The minimum length of statutory notice depends upon how long you have been employed:

continuous employment	*minimum notice*
less than 4 weeks	nil
between 4 weeks and 2 years	1 week
between 2 years and 12 years	1 week for each year of employment
over 12 years	12 weeks

If you are given less notice than that to which you are statutorily or contractually entitled, you can claim in the county court (sheriff court in Scotland) for wrongful dismissal.

You have to be paid during your period of notice even if you are on holiday, and your right to minimum payment continues if you are laid off due to lack of work or are incapable because of illness or injury. But if you breach your contract or take part in a strike during the notice period, you have no right to be paid from that time.

You may be offered wages in lieu of notice, but you have a right to refuse to accept if you prefer to work out your notice period. You get pay in lieu of notice free of tax; on the other hand, you cannot then claim unemployment benefit until the period of notice is over.

Leaflet no 14 in the Department of Employment employment protection series deals with *Rights on termination of employment*.

Even if given proper notice, you may still have grounds for claiming unfair dismissal.

unfair dismissal

Unfair dismissal is a technical concept. In order to get a remedy

- you must prove that you have been dismissed
- your employer must be unable to show that he had a reason for dismissing you that fell within the potentially fair reasons for dismissal
- your employer must have acted reasonably, in all the circumstances, in dismissing you for that reason.

dismissed?

The most obvious case of dismissal is termination of your contract of employment by your employer. It does not make any difference whether or not you are given notice, and includes the classic 'you are sacked'.

If you leave during your period of notice (perhaps because you have found another job), this still counts as being dismissed.

If you are employed on a fixed term contract, whether short or long, at the expiry of that term without renewal, you are dismissed. (But someone on a fixed term contract for one year or more may agree in writing to waive his or her rights to claim unfair dismissal when the term runs out and is not renewed.)

A woman who is not allowed to return to her work following pregnancy when she has declared her intention to do so is regarded as having been dismissed on the day she was due to return.

If your employer goes into liquidation or receivership, all contracts of employment are automatically terminated. This is deemed to be dismissal.

If you establish constructive dismissal – that is, having to leave your employment as a result of the employer's conduct toward you – you have been dismissed.

There are, however, several ways in which your contract of employment may come to an end which are not dismissal:

– resignation or termination of contract by mutual agreement
– mere warning of dismissal
– contract 'frustrated'.

Any type of contract is terminated by frustration when some unforeseen event, the fault of neither party to the contract, makes the contract or job either impossible to fulfil or radically different from what was originally intended. Crippling accidents, very serious illnesses, death, imprisonment, and the passage of a statute making that employment illegal can frustrate a contract.

reason for dismissal

If you have established that you have been dismissed, your employer has to show that his reason or principal reason for dismissal was not unfair and that, in the circumstances, he acted reasonably in treating it as a reason for dismissal.

Provided you have worked for the employer for 26 weeks, you are entitled to ask for a written statement from him giving particulars of the reasons for your dismissal. If the employer does not comply within 14 days of your request, or you think that the reasons he gives are inadequate or untrue, you can complain to an industrial tribunal. If the tribunal finds your claim well-founded, it can order the employer to pay you two weeks' pay, up to a maximum (of at present £260), and it can make a declaration about what it considers the employer's reasons were.

Three reasons for dismissal are automatically unfair:

- spent conviction
- pregnancy and confinement
- trade union membership or activity
  (a claim on this ground may be made without any qualifying period of employment)
  because
  you are a member of an independent trade union
  you take part in activities of your union at an appropriate time
  you refuse to join a non-independent trade union.

But your employer is not unfair in dismissing you for participation in a strike provided that he also dismisses all the others who took part. However, if he picks and chooses whom to re-engage and does not choose you, you may have a claim for unfair dismissal.

A claim for a remedy for unfair dismissal should be made to the industrial tribunal within 3 months of the effective date of dismissal (which is the date on which the notice expires or the last day the employee worked for the employer if he or she received pay in lieu, left during the notice period or received no notice).

If you are dismissed for trade union reasons, there is a special procedure for interim relief, so that wages continue to be paid and the contract continues, pending a full hearing of the case. You must make a special claim within 7 days, accompanied by a letter from your union official saying that he thinks you have been dismissed for a reason connected with the union. A hearing before an industrial tribunal chairman will be set up in a matter of days.

remedies

If you think you have been unfairly dismissed, you can claim reinstatement, re-engagement or financial compensation through an industrial tribunal. You can do this only if you have continuity of employment for 52 weeks and have worked 16 hours or more a week (if less than 16 hours a week but more than 8, you need continuity of employment for 5 years). But for a claim against an employer who has under 21 employees working for him the qualifying period is 104 weeks continuity of employment for anyone taken on after September 1980. But if at any time there are more than 20 employees, the qualifying period is the normal 52 weeks.

You cannot claim if you are dismissed when you are above the normal retiring age fixed by the contract or, if there is no such provision, over the age of 65 if a man and 60 if a woman.

In a case of unfair dismissal, an industrial tribunal can order

- reinstatement
  to be taken back to the same job and to be treated in all respects, including seniority, pay and pension rights, as though you had never been dismissed.

  Although this is supposed to be the primary remedy if you are unfairly dismissed, in fact it is rare. This is partly because most sacked employees do not want to return to their old employers. Moreover, it will not be ordered if it is not practicable or would be detrimental to the employer's business, or would inevitably lead to industrial unrest.

- re-engagement
  to be re-employed but not necessarily in the same job or under the same conditions and terms of employment.

  The new job, however, must be comparable and suitable and, as far as is reasonably practicable, as favourable as the previous position.

If your employer does not comply with a reinstatement or re-engagement order, you should apply for an 'additional' award for extra compensation; this is between 13 weeks' and 26 weeks' pay. If the dismissal was due to discrimination or trade union membership or activities, the additional award is between 26 and 52 weeks' pay. These additional awards are at the discretion of the industrial tribunal.

If you hope to be reinstated or re-engaged, do not delay in making your claim. The tribunal will not take into consideration the fact that your employer has engaged a permanent replacement for you unless your employer can show that he engaged the replacement after a lapse of reasonable time without hearing from you that you wished to be reinstated or re-engaged, or that it was not reasonably practicable for him to arrange his business otherwise.

compensation
This normally consists of two components, a basic award and a compensatory award.

– *basic award*
irrespective of whether your dismissal has caused you any loss, the award is based on the factors of age, wage and length of continuous employment with that employer or any associated or predecessor employer, up to a maximum of 20 years:

for a man aged 41 to 64 and a woman aged 41 to 59
1½ weeks' pay for each full year of employment within those years and 1 week's pay for each full year of employment from age 22 to age 40, and ½ a week's pay for any year before age 22

for a person aged 22 to 40
1 week's pay for each full year of employment within those years and ½ a week's pay for each full year of employment before then

for a person below the age of 22
½ a week's pay for each full year of employment.

A week's pay is taken as your normal gross pay at the time of notice of dismissal, or £130 (in 1981), whichever is less.

The maximum basic award is therefore £3900 (1½ × 20 × £130), which could be made to a man aged over 61. The maximum a woman could receive is £3770—because of her earlier retirement age, a woman can qualify for no more than 18 years at 1½ weeks' pay plus 2 years at 1 week's pay.

The calculations are based on full years; anyone who is a threshold age (21/22 or 40/41) at the time of dismissal, counts as being the lower age. For a person within a year of retirement age, the total entitlement is reduced by one-twelfth for each complete calendar month after his 64th or her 59th birthday, so that at the age of 65 (or 60) no basic award is due.

A basic award may be reduced if you unreasonably refused an offer of reinstatement or because of your contributory fault.

– compensatory award

This is an additional award to compensate you for any loss as a result of the dismissal. If you have suffered no loss, you can claim nothing under this heading.

The elements of the compensatory award are normally:

- the net-of-tax earnings you would have received from that job since the date of dismissal up to the tribunal hearing (the award will be reduced by the amount of any earnings from another employment during that time)
- any future net earnings you would have received: the amount is based on how long you are likely to be unemployed, and whether you are likely to have to take a job at a lower wage than your previous employment. Also taken into account are any increases in wages you would have received in the near future in your old job.
- loss of fringe benefits to which you would have been entitled in your

old job by contract or established custom (for example, a company car). Non-contractual bonuses such as Christmas gifts cannot be claimed.

- expenses in looking for work
- loss of pension rights: the calculations here may be very difficult. It may be more appropriate to base the sum lost on the amount of contributions made or, particularly for someone approaching retirement age, on how much it would cost to buy an annuity to produce the pension which you have lost. The tribunal will take into account your chances of getting pensionable employment in the future.
- loss of employment protection in a new job: it will take you 52 weeks to build up continuous employment sufficient to found a claim for unfair dismissal in the next job and 104 weeks for redundancy payment, for instance. The entitlement to both will also be correspondingly less. A fairly nominal sum, perhaps between £30 and £50, may be awarded in this respect.
- the manner of the dismissal: only if this is going to make it more difficult to get a comparable job.

There is a statutory limit on the amount of a compensatory award: at present, this is £6250.

The amount of compensatory award you actually receive will have deducted from it any unemployment (or supplementary) benefit you have had in the interim, which the employer has to pay back to the Department of Employment (until he has done so, you are not paid any of the compensatory award). Where there is an element of future loss of earnings in the award, you cannot claim unemployment benefit for any period covered by the award within the first year after the termination of employment.

An award may be reduced because of contributory fault or a failure to mitigate loss.

contributory fault

If the dismissal was to any extent caused by or contributed to by an action of the employee, compensation may be reduced by such an amount as the tribunal considers just and equitable. If you have, in effect, provoked your own dismissal, your compensation may be reduced by, say, 50 per cent. In extreme cases, your award may be reduced to nil, but this is only likely to be in a case where the unfair dismissal is very technical, or where something has come to light after dismissal indicating that dismissal would be justified for some other reason.

mitigation
A reduction will be made if you fail to take reasonable steps to get another job. It is important, therefore, that you keep a written record of jobs you apply for and the reasons you did not get them, to put before a tribunal.

wrongful dismissal
You can claim wrongful dismissal at common law if you are dismissed in breach of one of your contractual terms: for example, because your contract should last for a fixed period and you were sacked before that time elapsed, or you were dismissed without your entitlement to notice. A claim for wrongful dismissal has to be taken to the county court (sheriff court in Scotland). The court can award whatever damages are appropriate—no statutory amounts are laid down.

You may make a claim for wrongful dismissal in a situation where there has been a breach of contract but

- for some reason you are not entitled to claim unfair dismissal (for instance, you do not have a sufficient period of continuous employment)
- you are out of time to make a claim for unfair dismissal to an industrial tribunal, which must be done within 3 months; the time limit for a wrongful dismissal claim is 6 years
- you are earning so much that the upper limit laid down for compensation for unfair dismissal is below what you can expect to get for wrongful dismissal. For instance, you can recover loss of pay up to what would have otherwise been the end of your contract. This is subject to mitigation so that you cannot be compensated for any loss which you could have avoided by reasonably looking for other work.

Taking a case to the county court (sheriff court in Scotland) can take longer than a claim to an industrial tribunal, and can be more expensive – much more so in the High Court for a claim over £2000 (or if in Scotland you take a claim for over £500 to the Court of Session).

If you lose an action in the civil courts, you are most likely to have to pay the successful party's legal costs. In industrial tribunal claims, costs are awarded only in limited circumstances.

Relevant booklets published by the Department of Employment include *Fair and unfair dismissal* (a guide for employers) and *Employment Act 1980* (an outline).

industrial tribunal

There are about 70 industrial tribunals sitting every day in all parts of the country. A tribunal consists of a chairman, who is a lawyer, and two independent lay members, one from each side of industry.

Most applicants at tribunals are not legally represented. Legal aid is not available for representation before an industrial tribunal but there is free legal advice under the so-called 'green form' scheme ('pink' in Scotland) for those whose financial resources are below set limits. This entitles you to £40-worth of the time of any solicitor who takes on legal aid work. Alternatively, many solicitors will give anyone, regardless of means, a half-hour's interview for a fixed fee (currently, £5). If you do not know a solicitor experienced in employment law, the Law Society's Legal Aid Solicitors List (the Directory of Legal Services in Scotland) published annually and available in public libraries, citizens advice bureaux and similar information points, indicates the type of work undertaken by the solicitors listed.

Some people get help with their cases from a law centre or citizens advice bureau or a knowledgeable friend. If you are a member of a trade union, you should ask your union for advice and assistance.

conciliation

The regional office of the Advisory Conciliation and Arbitration Service (ACAS) receives a copy of every application made to an industrial tribunal. The conciliation officers of ACAS have a statutory duty to try to settle a complaint before the case has to come to a tribunal hearing.

In all cases, the conciliation officer makes an initial approach offering his services to the employer and to the claimant. His role is to help the parties to establish the facts and to clarify their views, not to impose his own views on the merits of the case. The conciliation officer usually deals with the claimant and the employer separately and acts as an intermediary, carrying settlement terms from employer to employee. However, there is no need to feel that an offer has particular authority because the conciliation officer puts it to you.

Information given to the conciliation officer is confidential and cannot be quoted in evidence before a tribunal without the permission of the person who gave the information.

Even without a formal application being made to the tribunal, the conciliation officer can be asked by either the employee or the employer to help to settle a complaint.

If a settlement is reached through the conciliation officer, this will be reported to the industrial tribunal and can become the basis of an enforceable order. But a settlement reached through a conciliation officer will normally prevent you from pursuing your complaint before the tribunal at a later date.

Leaflets about ACAS, including addresses of regional offices, are available free from the ACAS head office, Cleland House, Page Street, London SW1P 4ND, and also a booklet on the conciliation procedure in complaints by individuals to industrial tribunals. In Northern Ireland, the Labour Relations Agency carries out a similar function to ACAS.

When deciding whether or not to take a former employer to a tribunal, bear in mind the time and possible cost in relation to what you might be able to get if successful. It also means energy diverted when you should be job hunting—not to speak of the possible ill-will generated, which could work against you when a future employer contacts the ex-.

But if you do decide to go ahead, do not delay too long: there are time limits.

time limits

There is a time limit for making a claim for unfair dismissal (and for the various other employment rights), so you should not delay in putting in your claim, even if you have brought in ACAS or even if you are still using grievance procedures or are awaiting the outcome of a civil court case. If you do not apply in time, your case will not be heard.

Industrial tribunals have discretion to allow a claim to be made later than these limits (*except * in table opposite*) but only if it is considered not to have been reasonably practicable for the application to have been made sooner. Tribunals interpret this strictly: you would be excused only if you did not know of the time limit and there was no good reason for you to enquire.

Provided you have put in your application within the stipulated time, if you subsequently realise that your case is not as watertight as you had thought, you can withdraw it. Or, if more time is needed for negotiation or preparation of your case, the secretary of the industrial tribunals can be asked to postpone or adjourn your case to a later date.

CLAIM	TIME LIMIT FOR APPLYING TO TRIBUNAL
written statement of terms of employment	13 weeks of starting employment (if no longer doing that job, within 3 months of its termination)
itemised pay statement*	any time while in the employment or within 3 months of its termination
time off for public or trade union duties and activities	3 months from date of refusal
guarantee pay during short-time or lay-off	3 months from the day for which payment not received
pay on suspension on medical grounds, or retained job	3 months from first date for which payment claimed or 3 months from the date of dismissal
maternity pay	3 months from the end of the payment period
time off with pay for antenatal care	3 months from the appointment
job when wishing to return to work after pregnancy	3 months from the day on which it was intended to resume work
pay equal to that of an employee of the opposite sex doing like or equivalent work*	any time while doing job; 6 months after date of ceasing to do that job
discrimination on grounds of colour, race, nationality or sex	3 months from the date of the act of discrimination
exclusion or expulsion from a trade union	6 months from refusal or expulsion
written statement of reasons for dismissal	3 months from date of termination of employment
reasonable time off with pay to look for work or training during redundancy notice period	3 months from the day for which payment not received
payment on redundancy	6 months from date employment ceased
back pay and/or occupational pension contributions on insolvency (when Secretary of State has not paid in lieu)	3 months from the date of the Secretary of State's decision
protective award (application made by trade union)	3 months from the last day for which employer failed to pay
compensation for unfair dismissal	3 months from date of termination of employment
interim relief on dismissal for trade union activities*	7 days of effective date of termination

tribunal procedure

The first stage is an originating application, the document in which you state what you are claiming before the tribunal. It is usually most convenient to use the simple official IT1 form which is available from jobcentres and other Department of Employment offices and also from trade union officials. The form includes notes for applicants' guidance. A booklet (ITL1) is issued with IT1 giving guidance for those concerned in industrial tribunal proceedings.

You do not need to use this IT1 form, however. If you do not, you should state clearly

- your name and address
- the name and address of the person or company you are complaining against (the respondent)
- what you are claiming for: for example, redundancy payment or unfair dismissal compensation
- the grounds of your claim: for example, 'I was unfairly dismissed because . . .'

You must send your originating application to the Secretary, Central Office of the Industrial Tribunals, 93 Ebury Bridge Road, London SW1W 8RE (in Scotland, St Andrew House, 141 West Nile Street, Glasgow G1 2RU).

Your opponent has 14 days to submit his reply to your application (usually on a form IT3 'notice of appearance by respondent'), a copy of which is sent to you. The fortnight may be extended with the consent of the industrial tribunal.

The Equal Opportunities Commission's free booklet *How to prepare your own case for an industrial tribunal*, mainly intended for sex discrimination and equal pay claims, can be useful for other claims too.

documents and witnesses

If your employer's reply contains vague or ambiguous claims or anything you do not understand, you can ask for 'further particulars', so that you know exactly what allegations you have to meet. Your employer might ask the same of you.

If you want to amend your application, you can do so with the consent of the industrial tribunal. Similarly, your employer can amend his reply.

You may need documents in your employer's possession (and vice versa) to prove your case. (This is called 'discovery'.) The initial approach should be directly to the other side. If the other side refuses further particulars or discovery, the industrial tribunal has discretion to order these. Refusal to comply may result in a fine of up to £100.

You can call witnesses to support your claim. It is better that your witnesses come voluntarily, but if your case depends on having a particular witness who is unwilling to attend, you can apply to the industrial tribunal for a witness order, compelling him or her to appear. Each party can submit written representations as well as, or instead of, calling witnesses at the hearing.

before the hearing

The tribunal may hold a pre-hearing assessment (either on the application of your employer or on its own decision) to determine whether there is a sufficient case against the employer. It looks at your application and considers any representations in writing or by oral argument. The pre-hearing assessment lasts less than an hour, and you may not need to be present. If the tribunal states that it considers your application unlikely to succeed, this does not mean that you cannot go ahead. But if you do, you are at risk that an order for costs will be made against you.

You will get at least 14 days' notice of the date of the hearing, which will usually be about 3 months after you have submitted your originating application. If the proposed date does not give you enough time to prepare your case, you should write to the industrial tribunal, giving the reasons and asking for an adjournment.

You should make 6 copies of any documents you want to put before the tribunal so that you can give one to each of the tribunal members, one to your opponent, one to the tribunal clerk and keep one for yourself.

the hearing

Generally, the hearing is informal; the degree of formality or informality depends very much on the attitude of the tribunal chairman. Some chairmen explain the procedure fully as it goes along.

If you are not legally represented and your employer is, the industrial tribunal chairman may actively assist you – for example, with cross-examining the witnesses of the other side.

You should make a short opening address to the tribunal, outlining the nature of your case. You are likely to be your own most important witness. Tell your story simply, clearly and in a logical order. You can tell the tribunal not only what you yourself saw, heard or felt but also what someone else told you he saw, heard or felt. You are not confined to the grounds of complaint you set out in your originating application; however, if you have changed your story, any differences are likely to be challenged by your opponents.

The questions you ask any witnesses you call should be designed to bring out their factual knowledge of events. You should try not to ask questions which presuppose the answer and you should not invite your witnesses to give their opinion, or to speculate on matters which they could not know anything about.

Then the other side cross-examines you and/or your witnesses, putting to you any matter on which his evidence differs from yours. After cross-examination, you may be able briefly to re-examine a witness to re-establish your side of the story. After this, the members of the tribunal may ask some questions of their own.

After the other side has gone through the same process of examination, cross-examination, re-examination and questioning by the tribunal, each of you makes a closing speech saying why the industrial tribunal should decide in your favour.

The chairman gives the decision of the tribunal usually on the same day as the hearing. In a complicated claim, however, the decision may not be communicated until some weeks later.

after the hearing

If the finding is in your favour, and payment is ordered, the tribunal will specify the exact sums due to be paid. Payment should be made direct to you by the (ex-)employer as soon as is reasonable after the decision has been notified to you both, without further need to refer to the tribunal.

The document you get confirming the tribunal's decision is accompanied by information on enforcement proceedings, where necessary. In Scotland, if payment has not been received within 42 days, a request to enforce should be made to the secretary of the tribunals without further delay.

If you have drawn unemployment or supplementary benefit in the period between dismissal and the hearing, payment of the award will be delayed until the benefit authority has recouped from the employer whatever amounts you have had.

An order that you are to be taken back by the employer to take up your own or a similar job will state what rights and privileges are to be restored, and the date by which the order must be implemented.

If you have been unfairly dismissed and are subsequently reinstated, the intervening weeks are automatically counted in for continuity of service. If you are re-engaged, the tribunal decides about this.

If the employer will not re-engage you on the terms agreed or will not re-engage or reinstate you at all, you can go back to the tribunal and claim an 'additional' award (maximum at present £3380 – that is, 26 weeks at £130) as well as a basic and compensatory award. (If the reason for your claim was unfair dismissal on grounds of discrimination or trade union activity, the maximal 'additional' award is at present £6760 – that is, 52 weeks at £130.)

review

If you want to apply for a review of the decision by the industrial tribunal, you must do so within 14 days of the decision being sent to you. Apply in writing to the secretary of the tribunals in the region where your case was heard. The only grounds for a review are that

- one party did not know of the hearing
- a clerical error led to a wrong decision
- there is some decisive new evidence, the existence of which could not reasonably have been known to you or foreseen at the time of the tribunal hearing
- if there were no review, there would be a miscarriage of justice.

The chairman of the tribunals may refuse your application for a review if it has no reasonable prospect of success.

appeal

An appeal can be made to the Employment Appeal Tribunal to reverse the tribunal's decision – but only on a point of law. Where the claim alleged unreasonable exclusion or expulsion from a trade union, however, an appeal to the EAT may be made on a question of either fact or law.

You should take legal advice, preferably specialist, before mounting an appeal.

Redundancy

Redundancy is dismissal due to the disappearance of your job. The statutory definition is that

- the employer has ceased or intends to cease to carry on business altogether, or to cease carrying it on in the place where you were contracted to work
- the requirements of the business for employees to carry out work of the particular kind in which you were engaged have diminished or ceased either altogether or in the place where you were contracted to work.

A person who has been made redundant is entitled to redundancy payment from his employer (who can get back a percentage of such payments from the government's redundancy fund).

The statutory redundancy payment is calculated in the same way as for the basic award for unfair dismissal, with the maximum of £130 per week for each year of employment up to a maximum of 20 years. You are entitled to a written statement of how your employer has worked out the sums. (He can be fined £20 for refusing such a statement and £100 each time he refuses again.) Your entitlement to redundancy payment may be reduced if you leave during notice of redundancy and your employer has requested you in writing to remain for the full period of notice. Redundancy payment is paid tax free and does not affect entitlement to unemployment benefit.

You are not entitled to the statutory redundancy payment if

- you are over retirement age (65 years for a man, 60 for a woman)
- you have less than 104 weeks' continuous employment with that employer or an associated employer
- your working hours have been less than 8 hours a week
- your working hours have been between 8 hours and 16 hours a week for less than 5 years with the same employer.

An employer's arrangements for redundancy provisions may be more generous than the statutory ones, and these exclusions may not apply.

alternative job

Your employer does not have to make a redundancy payment if he has made an offer of suitable alternative employment which you have unreasonably refused. The offer

- must be made before your old contract or your notice period runs out
- must be for employment by your old employer or an associated or successor employer
- must be sufficiently specific in its terms so that you know exactly what the new situation involves.

Whether it was reasonable or unreasonable of you to refuse the position offered depends on the suitability of the job, the pay, and factors personal to yourself. such as inconvenience and expense involved (for instance, shiftwork thirty miles away) or loss of status (for instance, headmaster to supply teacher).

You are allowed to have a go at the new job for a trial period (4 weeks, but longer by written agreement between your employer and yourself) in order to make up your mind about it, without losing your rights to a redundancy payment.

being made redundant

You should check that the redundancy payment proposed by your employer meets the statutory requirements. The Department of Employment publishes a booklet called *The Redundancy Payments*

Scheme which gives full details and includes a ready reckoner for calculating redundancy payments. There is also a summarising leaflet of information for employees. Both are available free from jobcentres and unemployment benefit offices.

The length of notice for redundancy is the same as for ordinary dismissal, whether by contract or statutorily.

The employer must pay you your normal salary up to the date of the expiry of the notice, even if he has asked you to leave before then and you do leave early at his request. But to preserve your right to redundancy payment, be careful to distinguish between just being warned of a forthcoming redundancy and being given your notice of redundancy. Unless and until you are told the particular date on which you will be made redundant, you should stay at work; otherwise, you will be found to have resigned rather than have been dismissed. (Being able to prove that you have been dismissed is a necessary condition to claim a redundancy payment at an industrial tribunal, if that should become necessary.)

Any request about varying the date of departure should be made in writing; if the employer objects, in writing, he may contest his liability to pay redundancy payment.

Also, if the employer has given you advance notice longer than that required by law or by your contract, and you want to leave earlier, wait until the statutory or contractual notice period starts before you ask to leave early. For example, if your due notice period is 4 weeks and the employer tells you that you will be made redundant on a date 6 weeks ahead, wait until 2 weeks have gone by and then say that you would like to leave in, say, a week's time (a week being the minimum statutory notice an employee has to give an employer).

Your contract with your employer may provide for severance pay or compensation better than the statutory redundancy payment. If you are made redundant without notice, you will be entitled to payment in lieu of the notice period set out in your contract. So, if your contract entitles you to 6 months' notice, you should be paid in lieu of notice a sum equivalent to 6 months' gross salary. In addition to any statutory or contractual redundancy payment, your employer may make you a voluntary (ex gratia) payment.

Employees without the statutory rights

ON UNFAIR DISMISSAL	TO REDUNDANCY PAYMENT
if woman aged 60 or over, if man aged 65 or over, or if over normal retiring age for job*	if woman aged 60 or over if man aged 65 or over
if less than 52 weeks' continuous service with same employer* or less than 104 weeks' continuous service since 1 October 1980 with firm employing fewer than 21 people throughout that time*	if less than 104 weeks' continuous service with same employer
if working less than 16 hours a week*†	if working less than 16 hours a week†
if directly employed by husband or wife	if directly employed by husband or wife
if ordinarily working outside Great Britain	if employed as a domestic servant in private household of close relative
on expiry of fixed term contract for 1 year or more where right to claim if not re-engaged at end of contract is excluded	if ordinarily working outside Great Britain (unless on day of dismissal at work here)
if on strike at the time (unless victimised)	if employed by government of overseas territory
if exempt because of special dismissal procedure agreement	on expiry of fixed term contract of two years or more where right to claim if not re-engaged at end of contract is excluded
	if exempt because employment covered by special redundancy arrangements

* except when dismissed because of trade union activities

† unless more than 8 hours a week for at least 5 years with same employer

The report on *Employment law* in *Money Which?* June 1981 includes what action to take if things go wrong.

rights on redundancy

Any employee with over two years' service who is given notice of redundancy is entitled to reasonable time off to look for new employment or make arrangements for training. If the employer refuses to give paid time off, a claim should be made within three months to an industrial tribunal who can award up to a maximum of two-fifths of a week's pay.

If you are entitled to redundancy pay, you do not usually have to go through any special claim procedure for the employer to make the payment. But if there are any problems, delays or inadequate payment, the onus is on you to claim the payment (in person or by letter, if necessary) from

1 the employer
2 his receiver or liquidator, if under receivership or being wound up
3 his personal representatives if he has died
4 an industrial tribunal within 6 months of your dismissal, if all else fails.

The procedure for the industrial tribunal is the same as for an unfair dismissal claim, and so are the forms. The remedy is an order by the tribunal that the ex-employer pay you the statutory amount due to you. If you are claiming unfair dismissal as well as redundancy, you can get only one basic award.

The industrial tribunal may reduce the amount of the payment and has discretion to withhold all of an entitlement if it accepts an employer's claim about the employee's misconduct after notice of redundancy had been given, or if the employee insisted on leaving early when the employer had properly requested him not to. If there is any doubt about your dismissal having been due to redundancy (for

instance, if your job has immediately been filled), you may be able to claim unfair dismissal. You should look at this particularly if you have been with the employer for over 52 weeks (when you can claim unfair dismissal) but not yet for 104 weeks (the minimum for redundancy payment).

selection for redundancy

The industrial tribunal will not investigate the rights and wrongs of a declaration of redundancy unless there is patent bad faith, but can make your employer reveal his criteria for selecting any particular employee for redundancy.

It may be held to be unfair where your employer has breached, without special reasons, an agreed procedure established for dealing with redundancies (such as last-in/first-out). More broadly, your selection for redundancy must be generally fair and reasonable. It will most likely be considered unfair if your employer had not consulted or warned you about the impending redundancy or your employer has not made any attempt to consider alternative employment for you.

Selection for redundancy is automatically unfair when it is on the grounds of trade union membership or activities.

Where an independent trade union is recognised at your place of employment for the purposes of collective bargaining, your employer must at the earliest opportunity on a declaration of redundancy consult the union whose members will be affected. Minimum periods are laid down for consultation according to the number of employees to be dismissed. No dismissals must take place during the consultation time. The employer must inform the trade union in writing of the reasons for the dismissals, the number and description of the workers to be made redundant (although he need not give their names) and the basis for their selection, and the proposed timing of the dismissals.

The remedy for failure to comply with these provisions is a strange hybrid of collective and individual aspects. The union has to take the complaint to an industrial tribunal but you as an employee are entitled to a 'protective award'. This means that your employer can be ordered to pay you wages for the period when consultation should have taken place. You can get this award even though you are not a member of the recognised trade union or of any trade union, and even if you have been employed for less than two years or are a part-time employee. The industrial tribunal assesses the appropriate payment in relation to the seriousness of your employer's default.

The relevant booklet in the Department of Employment employment protection series is no 2 *Procedure for handling redundancies*.

employer's insolvency

Redundancy often arises because of the insolvency of an employer. This can come about very suddenly – from one day to the next, even. The question then arises as to how you can make a claim for money owing to you.

Dismissal because of the employer's insolvency counts as redundancy, and you can claim redundancy payment in the usual way, provided you have a qualifying length of service with that employer.

When you are notified officially that your employer has become insolvent, whoever has been appointed as the 'relevant officer' to be the employer's representative (liquidator or trustee or receiver – usually an accountant) should send you the Department of Employment booklet *Employee's rights on insolvency of employer*, which outlines the procedure that will be followed.

There are three categories of debts owed to you as an employee which you may be able to claim in this situation (irrespective of your age or length of service).

1 Fully guaranteed debts

a. redundancy payment

b. payment in lieu of notice

This is for the statutory minimum period of notice (even if the notice period stipulated in your contract of employment is different) and is subject to a maximum (at present, £130 per week) even if your pay is more

c. a basic award (but not a compensatory award) ordered by an industrial tribunal on an unfair dismissal claim but not yet paid out

These debts are paid out of the government's redundancy fund (which will try to recoup them from the insolvent employer).

2 Partly guaranteed debts

a. arrears of pay up to a maximum of 8 weeks and £130 (at present) per week

b. up to 6 weeks' holiday pay, accrued in the 12 months before dismissal

c. guarantee pay (for any days when work is not provided)

d. pay due during suspension on medical grounds under health and safety regulations

e. pay due for time off to look for other work or for trade union activities

f. protective award ordered by an industrial tribunal but not yet paid.

These debts are paid out of the firm's assets. They are given preference over other claims on the insolvent company, but you may get only a percentage if there is not enough to go round all preferred creditors.

3 All other debts owing to an employee (such as payments over and above the statutory minima) are unsecured, and you are unlikely to receive more than a small percentage.

The liquidator should send you an application form on which to claim payment of relevant debts: IP2 to claim payment in lieu of notice, IP1 for all other claims. A claim for payment in lieu of notice cannot be made until the statutory period of notice has expired, and is likely to take a long time to process; an application for other payments should be dealt with fairly soon. Proof of debts will be required with the application form.

When the application form has been returned, the liquidator calculates the entitlements that seem due to you and sends you a form of agreement (IP5 or 5A) showing the calculated amounts. (Any payment in lieu of notice will have deducted from it unemployment or other social security benefits you received during that period.) Once you have agreed the amounts and the claim has been cleared by the Department of Employment, the liquidator will send you the due amount, deducting any tax and employee's national insurance and occupational pension contributions for which you are liable.

under notice of redundancy

Employers vary as much in the way in which they handle dismissals – especially redundancies – as do employees in their reaction to dismissal. Some employers announce redundancies well in advance (or start rumours) so that the actual severance comes as no surprise and is often a relief after the strain of waiting. Other employers believe in the 'instant death' approach.

Both approaches can be traumatic in their own way. The feeling that colleagues you have been close to have actually been planning your redundancy 'behind your back' can cause resentment and mistrust. The fact that you – or more precisely your job – was selected and not someone else can make you bitter. Simply the shock of having your basic financial security suddenly withdrawn can have a strong emotional and sometimes physical reaction.

It will help you come to terms with your new circumstances if you can recognise in yourself any of the usual shock symptoms:

- complete apathy and lack of desire to do anything (even get out of bed)
- the exact opposite, when you have an urge to be frantically active and 'busy'
- a strongly focused dislike of one person – your old boss or a colleague who 'survived'.

Sometimes these symptoms are physical:
- a major change in your eating or drinking habits
- tendency to body and head aches
- total lack of energy.

Most of these symptoms will disappear within hours or days but if they continue for more than a few days you might be wise to talk to your doctor.

After you have received notice, you may be faced with making a choice of leaving immediately with pay in lieu of notice, or working for, say, all or part of the notice period.

If you do not feel uncomfortable about it, you may prefer to stay at work. There is considerable benefit in seeking a new job while still actually in employment. However illogical it may seem in the light of the present extent of unemployment, employers prefer that their potential recruits are not actually out of a job.

If you are one of a group of employees made redundant in your firm, get together with the others to set up a resettlement organisation or working party with the employer's help. If there is a good personnel department, the manager should have persuaded the firm to earmark resources to help those whose employment is to be ended.

The financial arrangements relating to redundancy and notice payments will play a large part in any discussion you have with your employer. He may not have experienced making people redundant before and may not have thought through the effect such a situation can have on individual employees. It may be that because of cost, or the problem of creating precedents, he will find difficulty in agreeing to much variation from statutory amounts or the basic terms of his scheme. However, the employer may be feeling professional or personal discomfort at the situation, and may consequently be receptive to suggestions for ameliorating the position.

The employer can help by

- allowing you time off for interviews (he is under some statutory obligation to do so, anyway, but persuade him to be generous)
- giving you assistance with travel costs and other interview and job hunting expenses
- changing the termination date to allow an anniversary (either of age or reckonable service) to affect what you are eligible to receive or your pension arrangements
- writing on your behalf to other organisations (the personnel officer

could use his or her own professional contacts in other companies and organisations, to check on employment possibilities)

- allowing you typing, photocopying, telephone and office facilities for job hunting
- advising on preparing a curriculum vitae
- putting you in touch with a reputable career counsellor and perhaps paying the fees
- sponsoring you for a re-training or development course
- giving you advice or paying for you to obtain advice on your occupational pension rights and alternatives.

You will have to negotiate about the non-salary benefits which you may have enjoyed, such as

- company car
  – will you be allowed to use it during your notice period (whether you actually work out your notice or not)?
  – will the employer sell it to you at less than its market or basic value (but beware tax implications and the insurance premium)?

- private health insurance
  – can you be kept in membership of a group scheme until the next renewal date? or until you take up new employment?
- life insurance
  – will cover for death in service continue for any time after you leave (to avoid any gap until you can be covered under the scheme of a new employer)?
- company loan
  – how long before you have to repay, and how (in a lump sum or by instalments)?
  – can you continue the loan but at a different interest rate?

No matter what your feelings are, try to leave without recriminations if for no other reason than self-interest. Whether or not in applying for other jobs you give this employer as a referee, potential employers are likely to check with him.

It can be helpful to check or negotiate with your employer exactly what he would say about the circumstances of your departure: it will not help you if you say one thing to potential future employers and your last employer does not support this in a reference.

If you can, arrange a leaving interview or formal farewell with your boss (the more senior the better) and establish that he will support you in your job hunting, and will give helpful replies to enquiries – but do not rely too much on this.

If the company is going into liquidation or moving, ask for a written reference because later there may be no one left who knows you.

volunteering for redundancy

Sometimes an employer offers the opportunity to his staff to volunteer to become redundant. Volunteering for redundancy once the employer has given notice of redundancies does not affect your right to redundancy payment.

Even if the possibility is attractive to you, you should not rush to volunteer; indicate that you might be interested, without committing yourself, and get more details of the scheme and the provisions being offered.

First, you should clarify to yourself what would be your purpose in volunteering, and discuss fully at home how redundancy would affect you and your family:

- what would your level of income be, and how would that affect you and yours?

- would redundancy be an opportunity to change course – for example, to move home or into a different career – and would the redundancy money you get be sufficient for you to do this?

Your employer is likely to be seeking some advantage to himself through voluntary redundancies, so what he is offering should be not just equal to the statutory requirements he would have to meet if he enforced redundancies but ought to be better, as an inducement to volunteers. Timing can be important and, in particular, may affect your pension:

– if you are not to be offered an immediate pension but one deferred to your normal retirement date, will your paid-up pension be increased regularly?

The trustees of the pension scheme may have some discretion to provide you with better than normal benefits, provided the company is prepared to pay an appropriate amount into the fund. You would become a 'special' member, with a better pension than the scheme rules allow for other members. For example, if deferred pensions are normally frozen at the time an employee leaves, you may be able to negotiate for yours to be increased by a percentage each year up to retirement. Even if your employer is not prepared, or unable under the rules of his scheme, to provide you with special benefits, it is possible that he could provide a separate supplementary pension, or he may be prepared to make an ex gratia payment direct to you.

The employer should be generous towards his volunteers in other respects than the monetary ones and allow plentiful time off and travel expenses for job hunting (assuming you want to go on working) and other forms of assistance. Perhaps he can be persuaded to offer you tax planning advice, in order to minimise payments you may have to make or arrange for you to receive investment advice on any lump sum due to you.

It is easy to be tempted by the lump sum paid out on redundancy. It is not quite fool's gold, but in the present economic climate, it is advisable to think hard about the risks as well as the possible benefits, and to have a good plan for alternative employment, before finally confirming that you are willing to volunteer for redundancy.

tax

If you receive any large payments on termination of your employment – either compensatory or ex gratia – and these add up to more than £25,000 in all, tax will be due on any amount in excess of this, at half your top rate of tax.

Payments which are tax free provided they are in total within this £25,000 limit include

- redundancy payment
- pay in lieu of notice (provided it is not part of your contract of employment)
- compensation for loss of office
- any other payments that are – technically at least – unexpected (not a reward for services, but an ex gratia payment).

You may get a tax repayment if you paid income tax under PAYE during the tax year in which your job finished, because you will have received only a part of your personal and other tax allowances. The married man's allowance is £2145 (1981/82 tax year) so a monthly repayment of the tax of one-twelfth of this allowance could be due: at 30 per cent tax, this works out at nearly £54, so it is worth claiming. For a single person, whose personal allowance is £1375, the repayment would come to just over £34.

If you know you are going to be unemployed for less than four weeks, there is no need to claim: you will get any refund through your new employer deducting less tax from your salary for one month soon after you start work.

After four weeks of unemployment (or if your unemployment spans the end of the tax year), you should make a claim. You need to have form P45 which your previous employer should have given you when you left. This gives the tax code number which was used in taxing your earnings, the total amount of earnings from 6 April to the date you left the employment, the tax deducted from those earnings and the tax district which dealt with your tax affairs. You should take this form to your local inspector of taxes, together with claim form P50 which your previous employer should also have given you. (If he did not, get a copy from the local Inland Revenue office or PAYE enquiry office or unemployment benefit office.) Alternatively, send the two forms to the inspector of taxes named on the P45 form, marking your letter and envelope 'urgent: repayment case'.

An order for the repayment due to you should be received in two to three weeks; it can be cashed at a post office or paid into a bank. The tax inspector will also send you a form P52, which is a claim form for the period subsequent to the first claim period of 4 weeks, to be used if you are still unemployed. Further claim forms will be sent for subsequent periods until all repayments due to you have been received.

It is worth discussing your tax situation with the local tax office. Even if this is not the one with which you normally deal (that is, the tax office you had with your last employer), it can pass queries to your tax inspector. If your inspector is based in an office at some distance away, it is cheaper, and may be more effective, to get the local office to do any necessary telephoning than to do so yourself. If you live in the London area, you should go into a PAYE enquiry office; they are listed in the London telephone directory under 'Inland Revenue'.

financial commitments and arrangements

Unless you are very fortunate, there is almost certain to be a gap between losing one job and beginning another. Tell your family, friends and acquaintances clearly and unemotionally what has happened to your job, and what you are all going to have to do now. Better that children should have the facts from you than that they should learn bit by bit from overheard conversations – neighbours, grandparents talking – that you are unemployed. Even quite young children need to be told, so that they can adjust to facts rather than worry about something unspoken.

It would be a good idea to explain the situation fully to your bank manager as soon as you realise you may be out of work for some time. The sooner you take him into your confidence, the better – do not wait until you are in difficulty. Tell him what your plans are and get his advice about your finances generally and about how you should make use of any lump sum you may receive.

You may have debts outstanding on credit cards or hire purchase agreements. Do not hope for the best and ignore these commitments. It may be better to pay these with part of any lump sum payment you get, to save the high interest on such debts. (If you default, you may in future be blacklisted as a credit risk.)

If you have a mortgage, go and discuss the situation with the building society or bank manager. He may be able to suggest temporary adjustments such as paying interest only or extending the repayment term,

or an alternative arrangement such as changing to an option mortgage. But he is less likely to help you if the first he knows about your difficulties is when you fall into arrear with payments.

Your dwindling income may bring you to the threshold for a rent rebate or allowance (depending on whether you rent from the local authority or a private landlord) and for a rates rebate. (But not if you are getting supplementary benefit, because this takes account of rates and rent.) The local authority's housing or finance department or a citizens advice bureau can give you the relevant leaflets about getting money off your rent or paying less rates.

It is essential to prepare a budget, on a monthly basis, of where your money is going to come from and where it is being spent. This will show up where you can make savings, as well as giving you confidence that you can survive for x months without a drastic reduction in living standards.

Being unemployed

To get the advice and benefits that are available to you, you must go to an employment office or jobcentre to register for employment and to the unemployment benefit office to make a claim for unemployment benefit.

claiming unemployment benefit
There is no reason to feel ashamed or awkward about claiming unemployment benefit. It is your right, for which you have been paying into the national insurance scheme while you were employed. The staff at the unemployment benefit office deal with unemployed people every day of the week and therefore to them you are not unusual, and any awkwardness exists only in your own mind. The staff are used to people in your state and they may have become indifferent. The clerks at the counters facing a queue of worried and often antagonistic

unemployed under stress have a difficult job. If a clerk seems inconsiderate, or offhand, do not assume that it is directed personally at you.

Unemployment benefit offices are listed in the telephone directory: look under 'Employment, Department of'. The addresses are displayed at the post office, or a citizens advice bureau will be able to tell you where unemployment benefit offices are locally.

If you live more than ten miles from the nearest unemployment benefit office, you can make your initial claim by writing a note saying that you are now unemployed, and giving your name and address. Post it on the first weekday of your unemployment. You will be sent forms to complete.

Most unemployment benefit offices are open from monday to friday, between the hours of 9 and 4. If you can, choose an office that will be convenient for you to go to each week or fortnight while you are unemployed.

You should make your initial claim even if you are not yet eligible to be paid unemployment benefit.

You will need to take with you your P45 form which shows your national insurance number (or at least a note of your national insurance number).

You should be prepared to give information about your wife's or husband's earnings (if any); details of your dependants; details of any pensions or state benefits which you or they receive; also details of your last employment (unless that was more than 12 months ago).

You will need this information to complete the application forms: UB 461 for yourself, UB 534 (A, B, C or D) for an increase in benefit because of dependants. You will be given a leaflet (UBL 18) which explains what you must do when claiming unemployment benefit, initially and thereafter – and will have to declare that you have read it. Also available is the DHSS explanatory leaflet NI 12 *Unemployment benefit*.

Provided you satisfy the contribution conditions which require a certain amount of class 1 (employed earners) national insurance contributions to have been paid or credited and that you are fit for work and available for employment, you will normally qualify for benefit.

how much you get

The rates of benefit are given in a DHSS leaflet (NI 196) which is available from social security offices and unemployment benefit offices.

The 'benefit' consists of a flat rate payment (currently £20.65 per week; £22.50 from November 1981), with increases for eligible dependants (wife or husband or one other adult, and each child for whom you get child benefit). The increase for an adult dependant (at present £12.75 a week; £13.90 from November 1981) is not paid if the dependant earns more than that amount. Where it is the wife who has become unemployed, she cannot claim for the husband as a dependant unless he cannot work because of physical or mental infirmity.

You may also get an earnings-related supplement based on weekly earnings between specified limits in the tax year that ended in the April of the previous year. For instance, a supplement payable in 1981 is based on reckonable weekly earnings of between £19.50 and £135 in the 1979/80 tax year, with a maximum supplement of £14 a week.

The total benefit you get (flat rate benefit, plus increases for dependants plus supplement) cannot be more than 85 per cent of the reckonable weekly earnings on which your entitlement to supplement is based. If your flat rate benefit and increases for dependants come to more than 85 per cent of your reckonable weekly earnings, they can still be paid but you will not be entitled to any earnings-related supplement.

DHSS leaflet NI 155A (available at unemployment benefit offices) explains how earnings-related supplements are worked out, with a table showing maximum benefit related to earnings. This supplement is being abolished and will not be paid in any case where the period of interruption of employment starts on or after 3 January 1982. Where the period of interruption of employment starts before that date, the supplement can be paid after that date but only up to 30 June 1982.

Unemployment benefit is tax-free at present, but there are proposals to make it taxable from April 1982.

how you get it

When you first claim, you are given an unemployment benefit attendance card (UB 40) which will tell you at what time and on which day of the week you must report to the unemployment benefit office to claim benefit ('sign on'). It is important to go on the correct day, so as not to lose benefit.

Benefits are calculated on a daily basis, taking six benefit days to the week (saturday counts as a benefit day). If you do not claim your unemployment benefit on the first weekday of your period of unemployment, you may lose benefit: you do not qualify for the flat rate payment until the fourth day after you have registered for employment and claimed unemployment benefit. The first three days of a period of interruption of employment are called waiting days and you get no benefit for these days. The earnings-related supplement becomes payable on the thirteenth day.

Someone who has left a job voluntarily without good reason is disqualified from receiving unemployment benefit for a period of up to 6 weeks. It is for you to show that you had a good reason for leaving. The unemployment benefit office will ask your employer why you left your job. A copy of his reply will be sent to you for comment if it appears that you left voluntarily. It is sensible to agree with your employer what reason will be stated for your resignation so that both you and your employer respond similarly to enquiries, in order to avoid any payment of benefit being delayed by the need to clarify differing information.

You will be asked on your unemployment benefit claim form whether you have received (or expect to receive) any payment from an ex-employer in connection with the loss of your employment. The unemployment benefit office may also ask your employer for information about any payments made to you. If your employer makes you an ex gratia or redundancy payment, you can claim national insurance unemployment benefit straightaway. But if you have been given payment by your employer in lieu of notice or an award ordered by an industrial tribunal, you will not be paid unemployment benefit until the period covered by the employer's payment has expired. (And if your receive such a payment later, any unemployment benefit you were paid during that time may be deducted.)

There are also disqualifications where an employee was dismissed for misconduct or has refused an offer of suitable alternative employment.

money from other sources

Someone who is qualified to get unemployment benefit but is getting any other national insurance benefit, such as sickness benefit or widow's pension, will not be paid both but gets whichever benefit is the higher.

A person over 60 who is getting an occupational pension of more than £35 a week under a former employer's pension scheme will have his or her unemployment benefit reduced by 10p for every 10p by which the pension exceeds £35. (DHSS leaflet NI 230 deals with *Unemployment benefit and your occupational pension*.)

You should tell the unemployment benefit office as soon as you have done any work at all, whether paid or unpaid, or have received an offer of work. You may earn up to 75p a day without affecting your eligibility for unemployment benefit – but you should tell the unemployment benefit office anyway. Earnings are taken as the net amount, after deducting certain expenses in connection with the job – including, for example, reasonable travelling expenses, special equipment or clothing. (From November 1981, the 75p limit is due to go up to £2.)

For any day on which you earn more than the limit, your benefit will be stopped – but for that day only, irrespective of the amount you earn. So, if you do an odd day's work, even if you get paid £50 for it, you lose only the one day's unemployment benefit. Also you can earn as much as you like on a sunday because unemployment benefit is only for mondays to saturdays.

If you undertake any work which, even if unpaid, would prevent you from being available for work on any day, you will not be eligible for benefit for that day. You remain eligible for unemployment benefit provided you can show that you are still available for full-time employment and that, if you are working for an employer, the spare-time job is not the same as your usual main occupation. For example, an out-of-work plumber can do a part-time gardening job.

Provided you do a job for less than 8 weeks, you can renew your claim and get paid unemployment benefit again as soon as the job ends.

signing on

Payment is normally made fortnightly (one week in arrear, one week in advance) by girocheque posted to your home address. This can be paid into your bank account or cashed at a post office you have nominated.

Each time you sign on you have to go to the signing box allocated to you and there sign to testify that for each day covered by your claim you were unemployed and did not work, that you were able and willing to work but could not get any, and that your dependants' circumstances remain as stated in your original claim (if not, cross out this part of the declaration and write a statement of the new facts). When signing on fortnightly, you declare that for the days for which you get benefit in advance you have had no offer of work but that you will continue to look for and accept any suitable offer.

A man who is claiming an increase in benefit for his wife whose earnings fluctuate above and below the amount of the dependant's increase may be obliged to sign on every week.

If you know that you will not be able to attend on the specified day because of a good reason (for example, to go to an interview), you must give the unemployment benefit office prior warning. If you do not do so, you may lose benefit. Go on the very next day you can, rather than waiting until your next allocated day.

Someone who lives more than 6 miles away from the nearest unemployment benefit office need not go in person each time to the office, but can arrange instead to send by post a form declaring that he or she is still unemployed, countersigned by a householder, trade union official or an employee in the same industry, who is neither a relative nor receiving unemployment or supplementary benefit.

If you look for work in another area (under the job search scheme or on your own initiative), you should tell the unemployment benefit office before you go. If this is not possible, report to the unemployment benefit office in the new area as soon as you can.

You should tell the unemployment benefit office well in advance if you intend to go on holiday so that you can be told what to do about your claim for the period while you are away. If you go on holiday in the UK, you may be paid benefit on your return if you prove that you were nonetheless available for employment. You may have to give a holiday address where you can be contacted should a suitable job arise.

not getting unemployment benefit

You can be disqualified from receiving unemployment benefit for up to 6 weeks if you refuse to take a suitable job offered to you, unless you can show the authorities that you have good reason not to take that job. A job in your usual occupation is normally regarded as suitable but, after a time, you may be expected to take any other job where the wages and conditions are generally no less favourable. Your benefit also may be suspended if you fail to carry out any reasonable official recommendation made with a view to helping you find a suitable job, or do not accept an opportunity to take an approved course of training.

Your ability or willingness to work must not be hedged about with restrictions regarding the nature, hours, rate of pay, locality or other conditions of employment you are prepared to accept. You will not get unemployment benefit unless you can show that your restrictions are reasonable (for instance, because of your physical condition or the nature of your usual occupation). If the unemployment benefit office think that the restrictions you set may preclude any reasonable chance of your getting a job, you will be asked to give precise details of the work you are prepared to accept.

difficulties and disputes

The counter clerks at unemployment benefit offices are not instructed to deal with anything other than routine situations. They cannot advise whether someone will or will not receive benefit under this or that circumstance. Check as far as possible the details taken down about you: if a clerk makes any mistakes, you are the one likely to suffer.

Cross-check any information you are given – with posters, leaflets, other staff at the unemployment benefit office, co-claimants.

It is not easy to be sure that you are getting the right amount of benefit or whether you have claimed for all the extras you may have a right to. You may be able to check the calculation for the particular payments being made to you by reference to the relevant NI leaflets and evidence of your pay and national insurance contributions (from your P60 form). But if you are in any doubt, ask to see a supervisor at the unemployment benefit office (accommodation should be available for a private interview if you request it).

A supervisor should be able to explain the calculations, and the rules on which they are based, but does not have the authority to settle disputes. These are referred to an insurance officer, who may require more information from you.

When a question arises about your entitlement to benefit – for instance, because there is doubt about whether a rule is satisfied – you will receive a notification (UB 48) to tell you that the payment in question has been suspended while enquiries are being made. While a claim is being adjudicated, you are advised to continue to attend at the unemployment benefit office at the requisite times for claiming benefit. If the decision is then in your favour, you will get the arrears of payment. If not, you will be told the reason and of your right to appeal to a local national insurance tribunal within 21 days of the date of the decision, and how to set about it.

If dissatisfied with the tribunal's decision, you or your representative, which may be your trade union, can appeal to one of the national insurance commissioners, who sit in London, Edinburgh, and Cardiff.

for how long you can get benefit

Unemployment benefit can be paid for up to 312 days, which do not have to be consecutive, in any period of 'interruption of employment'.

Spells of unemployment (or sickness) that are separated from each other by not more than 8 weeks count as one period of interruption of employment, for the calculation of the total of 312 days' payment. This means, for example, that if you had claimed benefit for successive spells of unemployment (or sickness) and the spells were not separated by more than 8 weeks, the days in the first spell of unemployment would be added to days in the subsequent spell(s) of unemployment when working out whether you had drawn the full entitlement of 312 days.

After the 312 days, you cannot qualify again until you have worked as an employee for 13 weeks at least, not necessarily consecutive, working in each of those weeks for 16 hours or more.

An earnings-related supplement continues for up to 156 days in a period of interruption of employment. Any days for which you have received the supplement with unemployment benefit (or sickness benefit) in claims which link under the 8-week rule are added together.

Generally, someone claiming unemployment benefit is credited with national insurance contributions for complete weeks during which he or she can prove unemployment – this means having made a claim at an unemployment benefit office and continuing to attend and sign as unemployed. Contribution credits do not depend on being actually paid benefit. When your unemployment benefit comes to an end after 312 days, contribution credits may continue provided you prove that you are still unemployed by continuing to sign on at regular intervals.

supplementary benefit

About two weeks before you reach the end of your maximum of 312 days' payment of unemployment benefit, you get a formal letter (UB 684) notifying you that you will soon run out of unemployment benefit and suggesting that you may now wish to claim a supplementary allowance. If already receiving a supplementary allowance, this will be increased to cover the loss of unemployment benefit.

Anyone not in full-time employment whose weekly income falls below a statutory minimum can claim a supplementary allowance from the state. There are no national insurance contribution requirements: the criterion is your income level, not your national insurance record.

If your income is less than the statutory minimum level (known as your 'requirements'), you will be paid an allowance to bring your income up to your requirements. Requirements are based on a specific scale, designed to be enough to meet ordinary living expenses, which includes food, heat and light, replacing clothes, washing and cleaning expenses, and something for newspapers, TV licence and so on, but not big items such as bedding or furniture. There is also an amount for housing requirements, which covers rates and either rent or, for owner occupiers, mortgage interest payments, ground rent (feu duty in Scotland) and an allowance towards repairs and insurance.

If you have capital or savings of £2000 or more, you will not get supplementary benefit, however reduced your actual weekly income may be. So, if you have received redundancy payment, or been awarded generous compensation by an industrial tribunal, or been paid a handsome lump sum by your employer when you left, this will preclude you from claiming a supplementary allowance – until or unless there is no more than £2000 of it. The value of the home in which you live is disregarded in all the calculations.

When assessing your resources, the DHSS (which administers the supplementary benefits scheme) will disregard certain items of income. These include up to £4 a week of net earnings and up to £4 of a spouse's earnings; if you are a single parent, half of any net earnings between £4 and £20 a week is disregarded. In addition, up to another

£4 of the total of any other income may also be disregarded, such as voluntary payments from relatives or friends and tax refunds (but these may be regarded as capital). Child benefit, family income supplement and most national insurance benefits and pensions are not disregarded but taken into account in full when calculating your weekly income.

There are different 'scale rates' for assessing the requirements of different categories of people: householders, non-householders, lodgers, married couples (or cohabiting couples). For a couple, the claim must come from the man: a claim for supplementary benefit cannot be made by a cohabiting woman or married woman living with her husband.

The current rates are given in leaflet SB1 which includes a claim form and is available at social security offices, post offices and unemployment benefit offices. A simple explanation of how benefit is worked out (leaflet SB9) is sent to unemployed people when they have claimed.

The 1981 edition of the *Supplementary Benefits Handbook* (£2.40 from HMSO and available at local libraries) gives full details of claimants' rights and assessments of benefit.

Payment of a supplementary allowance is not usually made retrospectively, so do not delay claiming.

To qualify for a supplementary allowance, most people are required to be registered for work. If, for any reason, there is a dispute or a delay about your unemployment benefit and payment has been disallowed or temporarily suspended, the counter clerk at the unemployment benefit office should give you form B1 to claim a supplementary allowance (ask for it if he or she does not do so). The DHSS office will want full details of your circumstances in order to work out whether you are eligible for a supplementary allowance and for how much.

While a query on your entitlement to unemployment benefit is being investigated, any supplementary allowance you get will be reduced by up to a certain percentage (at present this works out at not more than £8.50). A similar reduction is made for up to 6 weeks if you are disqualified from receiving unemployment benefit because you left your last job without 'good reason' or lost it because of misconduct, or if you refuse a suitable new job also without good reason.

An unemployed person's supplementary benefit comes on a giro-cheque from the unemployment benefit office and continues to do so even when unemployment benefit payments cease.

While you are getting a supplementary allowance, you and your dependants are automatically entitled to various concessions on the NHS, such as free prescriptions, free dental treatment and dentures, free spectacles, free milk and vitamins for children under school age, free medicines and appliances as a hospital outpatient, and to free school meals. Also, you may ask for a specific single payment for an 'exceptional' need, which may be towards the cost of essential items of household equipment, or to help with extensive repairs or maintenance work.

You may also claim for necessary expenses on starting a new job, such as required clothing or tools, and fares for the journey to work for up to the first 15 days. And if you do not get paid straightaway on starting a new job, supplementary benefit may continue to be paid for 15 days. After 15 days, any supplementary benefit would be paid only in case of urgent need, and might be recouped from you afterwards.

signing off

Unemployment benefit ceases when you are no longer available for full-time work. When you have finally fixed yourself up with a new job, tell the unemployment benefit office. You have to complete the multi-purpose card (UB 40, which you were given when you first claimed unemployment benefit) giving the name and details of the new employer and the date of starting the new job.

Getting
a
new
job

check list for your new job

	points to note
job title	status, position, function
purpose of the job	minimum routine (flexibility allows job to be developed around own skills)
position in the structure	relationships: boss, subordinates, peers
place of employment	
working hours/days	flexibility/timekeeping normal, paid overtime, unpaid overtime, weekends etc; business entertaining in evenings or at home?
travel involvement	amount, times, places; class of travel; reimbursement; spouse as companion?
staying away from home	how often? reimbursement
working environment/office	sedentary/active; modern/archaic; shared/own; light, heating, noise
number and level of subordinates	supervisors, clerks, secretary; access to typing pool
authority	purchasing; hire/fire; will allow job to be done properly?
limitations	any restrictions on outside activities, paid or unpaid?
sickness	
– salary during illness	how much? for how long?
– medical expenses	private medical insurance scheme? family included?
– death in service	pension for spouse? children?

what you get	*points to note*
basic salary	
– starting	when first paid?
– payment dates	weekly/monthly; arrear/advance
– form of payment	cash/cheque/credit transfer
– review period	anniversary of start/specific dates
– review basis	performance? index-linked? (which index?)
other cash payments	bonus, commission, profit sharing, incentive, royalties; timing, basis?
car supplied	
– basis for type and model	
– basis for replacement	mileage/time/value
– basis for use	business, pleasure; wife drive? foreign holidays etc.
– payment of costs	maintenance, private petrol, parking, garage, tax, repairs, insurance, AA/RAC
– if out of action	car hire?
pension scheme	contributions required?
– basis	what percentage of (what) final pensionable salary?
– options on leaving	transfer/defer/refund
holidays	current year's arrangement?
– amount and basis	number of days per year; increases per year of employment?
– flexibility and choice	any limits? 'unused' days into next year?
– sabbatical	after how long? for how long?
expenses	
– amount of discretion	cash float? charge account?
– period of claim/payment date	immediate/weekly/monthly; claim in 7 days?
– basis of claim	actual costs (with bills)/fixed sum per item/fixed sum per period
– entertaining	including at home? reimbursement
– extras	newspapers, books, home telephone, postage

what you get	*points to note*
training	extent and type
– attending seminars, conferences	time off? who pays?
– release for external activities	lecturing, professional meetings
perks (not an exhaustive list)	
– cheap loans	for mortgage? bridging loan? season ticket?
– discounts for purchases	
– meals	subsidised? free?
– own car	garage/parking space? when used for business?
– pool car	provision of a driver?
– luncheon vouchers	taxable above 15p per day
– theatre, special event tickets	basis of allocation
– use of company assets	flat, holiday villa; office materials/equipment; professional advisers
relocation	moving house costs interim travel and accommodation (including family?)

when it ends	*points to note*
length of contract	fixed number of years or until terminated?
termination by employer	notice period and payments (salary in lieu of notice?)
– on redundancy	arrangements over and above statutory
restrictive clauses	restraint on operating in competition?
procedure in event of non-agreement	arbitration by?

Index

abroad, working, 28, 36, 68, 91, 135
accident at work, 104, 105, 118
accommodation provided, 83, 90, 96
additional award, 120, 131
additional voluntary contributions (AVCS), 68, 71
advertisements, job, 19, 28 *et seq*, 44
– by agencies, 23
– at jobcentres, 20
– for local government, 27
– replying to, 29 *et seq*
adviser
– civil service, 27
– at jobcentre, 21, 38
see also consultants
Advisory Conciliation and Arbitration Service (ACAS)
– and disciplinary practice, 112
– and industrial tribunal cases, 125, 126
age, 86, 120
– and basic award, 121, 135
– giving, 16, 31
– for job, 9, 18, 39, 40
– and national insurance contributions, 91
– and redundancy payment, 133, 135
– and retirement, 56, 57, 60, 64, 68, 103, 120, 121, 135
– and unemployment benefit, 152
agencies, employment, 18, 19, 20, 22, 33, 96
allowances, statutory
– for job search, 35, 51, 164
– maternity, 99, 102
– for rent/rates, 147
– while sick, 101, 102, 103, 104, 105
– tax, 87, 145
– while training, 16, 38
antenatal care, 98, 99, 127
application forms, 32, 33, 42
– for unemployment benefit, 150 *et seq*
applying for jobs, 16, 19 *et seq*, 33, 34, 71
– and c.v., 18, 25, 29, 32, 33
– direct, 18, 25 *et seq*, 34
– response to 33, 34, 92, 93
apprentices, 74, 91
armed forces, joining, 28, 39, 40
award *see* additional, basic, compensatory, protective

bank manager, 146
– as referee, 20
basic award, 83, 121, 139
bonus payments, 8, 63, 68, 83, 88, 92, 110, 123, 162
breach of contract, 109, 111, 112, 113, 124
– during notice, 117
British Institute of Management, 12
British Insurance Brokers' Association, 62
brokers, and pensions, 62, 63
building society manager, 146, 147

capital transfer tax, and pensions, 65
car, company, 52, 69, 77, 89, 90, 123, 142, 162
– parking own, 46, 70, 163
career
– assessing, 10 *et seq*, 144
– counselling, 11, 12, 142
– giving details of, 16, 17, 18, 32, 43
– prospects, 7, 10, 70
Careers Research and Advisory Centre, 23
Central Arbitration Committee, 86
Central Office of Industrial Tribunals, 128
check list, 161 *et seq*
citizens advice bureaux, giving information, 113, 125, 147,150
civil service jobs, 27, 28, 74
– applying for, 32
closed shop, 93, 94
clothes, 13, 70
– for interviews, 14, 45
– special for job, 69, 89, 153, 159
cold canvassing, 19, 25 *et seq*, 34
colleagues, 11, 14, 19, 20, 48, 49, 53
collective bargain, 74, 76, 79, 81, 86, 138
Commission for Racial Equality, 95, 97
commission, pay, 68, 73, 80, 83, 88, 162
Company Pensions Information Centre, 56
compensation
– claiming, 68, 127
– for discrimination, 97
– payments, 122, 123, 139, 145, 152, 157

– for unfair dismissal, 121 *et seq*
compensatory award, 122, 123, 152
conciliation, 125, 126
constructive dismissal, 111, 113, 118
consultants
– career, 11, 12, 142
– PER, 16, 21
– pension, 62, 63
– recruitment, 18, 21, 23 *et seq*, 31, 33
contacts, personal, 19, 20, 53
– using, 18, 19, 27
continuity of employment, 75, 82, 83
– and maternity rights, 99, 100
– and notice period, 117
– and redundancy payment, 123, 133, 135
– and strikes, 110
– and unfair dismissal claim, 120, 121, 123, 124, 131, 135
contract of employment, 37, 74 *et seq*, 107, 110
– breach of, 109, 111, 112, 113, 117, 124
– and continuity of employment, 82, 83
– ending, 77, 117, 118, 163
– and equality, 84, 85
– frustrated, 118
– and notice period, 7, 117, 118, 139
– and working hours, 78, 83
contracted-out pension schemes, 56, 57, 58, 60, 61, 63, 76, 91
contributory fault, 122, 123
convictions, spent, 98, 119
copyright, 77
criminal offence, 98, 115, 116
Corporation of Mortgage Brokers, 62
correspondence courses, 37, 70
costs
– saving, 35
– at industrial tribunal, 124, 129
Council for Accreditation of Correspondence Colleges, 37
counselling, 11, 12, 142
county court, claims in,
– and damages, 109, 112, 124
– for discrimination, 95
– for underpayment, 84
– for wrongful dismissal, 117, 124
Current British Directories, 26
curriculum vitae, 16 *et seq*, 33, 42
– detailed, 17, 18, 21
– help with, 12, 16, 18, 142
– presentation, 18
– sending, 18, 25, 29, 32, 33

death
– after retirement, 64, 65
– in service, 65, 143, 161
debts
– on employer's insolvency, 139, 140
– when unemployed, 146, 147
deferred pension, 9, 58 *et seq*, 66, 144
demotion, 113, 133
Department of Employment booklets, 74
– on continuous employment and pay, 84
– on dismissal, 124
– on Employment Act, 124
– on equal pay, 86
– on guarantee payments, 81
– on insolvency, 139
– on maternity rights, 98
– on medical suspension, 106
– on redundancy, 133, 134, 138
– on rights on termination, 117
– on union membership, 94
– on written statement, 76
dependants
– allowance for, 38, 87, 101, 102, 109, 150, 151, 153, 159
– and insurance, 40
– and pension, 59, 65, 161
see also spouse
DHSS leaflets, 55, 98, 101, 103, 105, 110
– and supplementary benefit, 157, 158
– on unemployment benefit, 150, 151, 152, 155
disciplinary procedures, 76, 92, 107, 110 *et seq*
discovery of documents, 128
discrimination, 94 *et seq*
– claiming, 96, 97, 127
– and dismissal, 120, 131
– and pay, 84 *et seq*
– permissible, 96
– racial, 92, 94 *et seq*
– sex, 85, 86, 94 *et seq*
dismissal, 110, 111, 112, 115 *et seq*

– constructive, 111, 113, 118
– date of, 119
– reasons for, 93, 95, 99, 118, 119
– wrongful, 112, 117, 124
dismissal, unfair, 73, 118 *et seq*, 137
– and maternity, 98, 99, 101
– reason for, 118
– remedies for, 83, 120, 127
– and trade union activity, 92, 93
disabled, 15, 20, 38, 91
disablement benefit, 104, 105
dispensations, tax, 89
disputes
– with employer, 68, 127, 163
– about unemployment benefit, 155, 156, 158
see also disciplinary procedures, strikes
doctor
– examination by, 43, 102
– note from, 99, 101, 102, 103
– report of, 115
– and spent convictions, 98
– suspending employees, 106

earnings
– after dismissal, 122
– national insurance limits, 91
– while sick, 102
– and supplementary benefit, 157, 158
– and unemployment benefit, 153
see also pay, salary
earnings-related
– pension, 56, 57, 62
– supplement, 102, 151, 152, 156
education, 10, 28
– contacts through, 19
– further, 37, 38
– giving details of, 16, 18, 30, 43
employee
– being an, 73 *et seq*
– and breach of contract, 112
– and discrimination, 94 *et seq*
– when dismissed, 117 *et seq*
– giving notice, 7 *et seq*
– leaving, 7 *et seq*, 77, 118, 143, 152
– paying national insurance contributions, 73, 87, 91, 99
– number of, 96, 99, 100, 107, 120, 136
– obligations of, 77, 81, 107
– when redundant, 132 *et seq*, 140, 141
– replacement, 106, 116, 121
– and tax, 87 *et seq*
employer
– and accident at work, 104, 105
– associated, 80, 82, 83, 85, 99, 133
– and breach of contract, 112, 113
– death of, 82
– deducting tax, 87, 88, 99
– and disciplinary action, 109 *et seq*
– and discrimination, 94 *et seq*
– and dismissals, 118 *et seq*
– giving written statements, 75 *et seq*, 110, 119, 132
– at industrial tribunal, 97, 128 *et seq*
– insolvency of, 118, 138 *et seq*, 143
– and insurance, 40, 73, 105, 107
– and national insurance contributions, 91
– and notice required, 7, 117
– obligations of, 73 *et seq*, 107, 108
– offering alternative job, 80, 99, 101, 115, 120, 133
– pension scheme, 8, 9, 54 *et seq*, 66, 71, 76, 152
– and perks, 52, 69, 88, 95, 122, 123, 142, 163
– previous, 11, 20, 59, 88, 126, 130, 143, 151, 152
– prospective, 17, 18, 23, 29, 31, 34, 35, 41, 53, 56, 67, 126, 143
– and redundancies, 132 *et seq*, 141
– and safety requirements, 73, 106, 107
– sick pay scheme, 101, 102, 103
– in small firm, 96, 99, 100, 107, 120, 135
– and wages councils, 84
employment agencies, 18, 19, 20, 22, 33, 96
Employment Appeal Tribunal, 131
Employment Medical Advisory Service, 106
employment office *see* jobcentre
employment protection rights, 37, 40, 73 *et seq*, 92, 106, 123, 135
– and hours of work, 78 *et seq*
Employment Service Division (ESD), 15, 20, 35

– leaflets, 20, 35, 36, 51
employment transfer scheme, 35, 36
Equal Opportunities Commission, 95 *et seq*, 128
equal pay, 77, 78, 84 *et seq*, 94, 127
executives, 15, 21
Executive Grapevine, 24
Executive Post, 21, 28
ex gratia payment, 134, 144, 145, 152
expenses, 52
– car, 69
– interview, 35, 41, 51, 141
– while job hunting, 35, 123, 141, 144
– paid by employer, 69, 162
– tax on, 88, 89
– while unemployed, 35, 157
experience, work, 10, 16, 17, 23, 29, 30, 32, 43
Extel Services, 42

files, keeping, 33, 53
– information on firms, 26, 29, 33, 34, 41, 42
final pensionable salary, 57, 59, 60, 62, 63, 64, 162
financial commitments, 146, 147
fines, 108, 110, 111, 129
fire precautions, 107
fit, keeping, 14
fixed term contract, 67, 76, 117, 118, 124, 135, 163
fringe benefits, 52, 69, 88, 95, 122, 123, 142, 163
– and tax, 89, 90, 142
frozen pension, 58, 60, 144
see also deferred
frustrated contract, 118
further particulars, 128

graduates, jobs for, 23
grievances *see* disputes
guarantee payment, 81, 109, 127, 139
guaranteed minimum pension, 57, 60, 61

hardship allowance, 105
headhunters, 25
health, 86, 115
– evidence of, 40, 43, 115
– insurance, 69, 90, 103, 143, 161
– at work, 99, 106 *et seq*
Health and Safety at Work Act, 106
– enforcement, 108
Health and Safety Executive, 108
holidays
– entitlement to, 52, 68, 69, 74, 76, 84, 162
– pay, 69, 74, 76, 84, 139
– and unemployment benefit, 154
hours of work, 52, 68, 70, 78 *et seq*, 161
– and lack of work, 80, 81
– and pay, 83
– qualifying, 98, 120, 133, 135
– and written statement, 75, 76
see also continuity of employment

illness, 101 *et seq*, 118
– industrial, 103, 104
– leave for, 69
– previous, 43
– pay during, 69, 76, 101, 117
implied terms, 74, 77, 78, 107, 111
index-linked pensions, 63
inflation, and pension, 8, 57, 59, 60, 62, 63, 64
industrial disease, 103, 104
– benefit, 104, 105
industrial tribunal claims
– applying, 125 *et seq*
– constructive dismissal, 112, 113
– and costs, 124, 129
– discrimination, 96, 97
– hearing at, 119, 129 *et seq*
– interim relief, 119
– non-equal pay, 86
– pre-hearing assessment, 129
– procedure, 128 *et seq*, 136
– redundancy payment, 81, 82, 134, 136 *et seq*
– remedies, 120 *et seq*, 139, 152
– representation at, 79, 97, 129
– review and appeal, 131
– time limits, 127

– time off, 108
– unfair dismissal, 112, 119, 124
– written statements, 76, 119
injury at work, 76, 82, 108
– benefit from state, 104, 105
– insurance for, 73, 107
– pay during, 117
Inland Revenue, 88, 89
– booklet on expenses, 90
– P2 form, 88
– P45 form, 88, 91, 145, 150
– P50 form, 145
– P52 form, 146
– P60 form, 88, 155
– inspector, 145, 146
– and pension limits, 62, 64, 71
– and tax coding, 88, 145
– and tax dispensations, 89
insolvency, employer's, 118, 136, 138 *et seq*, 143
Institute of Personnel Management, 24, 45
– recruitment code, 44, 45
insurance, 52
– for car, 142
– by employer, 73, 105, 107
– life, 40, 56, 67, 68, 143
– for medical treatment, 69, 90, 161
– permanent health, 103, 143
interim relief, 119, 127
interviews, 32, 41 *et seq*
– afterwards, 52, 53
– behaviour at, 12, 16, 47 *et seq*
– being asked to, 29, 30, 34, 35, 41
– civil service, 28
– clothes for, 14, 45
– with counsellor, 11, 12, 21
– expenses, 35, 41, 51, 141
– going to, 35, 46
– keeping notes on, 33, 52
– panel, 50, 51
– preparing for, 41 *et seq*
– with recruitment consultant, 23, 25
invalidity benefit, 103

job
– abroad, 28, 36, 135
– accepting, 67 *et seq*, 71
– alternative, 80, 99, 101, 115, 120, 133, 152, 154, 158
– applying for, 19 *et seq*, 35
– assessing new, 7, 10, 67 *et seq*, 92, 161 *et seq*
– capability for, 10, 38, 42, 115
– and continuity, 75, 82 *et seq*
– evaluation study, 85
– leaving, 7 *et seq*, 152
– offers of, 34, 51, 52, 54 *et seq*, 67
– part-time, 138, 153
– past, 10, 16, 17, 29, 43
– scope of, 67, 161
– starting, 70 *et seq*, 159
– temporary, 22
jobcentres, 15, 18, 20, 21, 28, 51, 134
– and jobs elsewhere, 35
– registering at, 15, 148
– and training courses, 38
job hunting, 19 *et seq*, 33 *et seq*, 141, 144
– in another area, 35, 51, 154
– organising, 12 *et seq*, 33, 35
– techniques, 12, 16
job library, 21
job search scheme, 35, 51, 154

Kelly's *Manufacturers Directory*, 26
Kemp's *Recruitment Handbook*, 24
Key British Enterprises, 26
Kompass Register, 26

lay-off, 81, 117
leaving job, 7 *et seq*, 152
legal aid and advice, 125
letters
– of application, 13, 26
– replying to adverts, 29 *et seq*
library, reference
– advertisements at, 27, 28
– books in, 23, 24, 26, 37, 42, 44, 158
– using, 25, 28, 29, 34
life insurance, 40, 56, 67, 68
liquidator, 138, 139, 143
loan, from employer, 69, 90, 143, 163

local government jobs, 27, 50, 51
lump sum, 73
– on death, 65
– for disablement, 104, 105
– and guaranteed pension, 65
– on redundancy, 144, 145
– on retirement, 64
– and supplementary benefit, 157
– using, 144, 146
luncheon vouchers, 69, 163

managers, 12, 15, 17, 21
Manpower Services Commission, 15, 35, 37, 51, 96
maternity, 98 *et seq*
– absence for, 82
– allowance, 98, 99, 102
– and dismissal, 98, 99
– leave, 100, 101, 127
– pay, 83, 99, 127
meals, allowance, 16, 68, 69, 163
medical appeal tribunal, 102
medical suspension, 83, 106, 116, 127, 139
medical treatment
– as employee, 69, 102, 115
– insurance scheme, 69, 90, 143, 161
misconduct, 102, 110, 111, 115, 116
– and unemployment benefit, 152, 158
mitigation, 124
money purchase pension schemes, 57, 58
mortgage
– loan from employer, 69, 90, 163
– payments, 146, 147, 157
moving house, 36, 69, 163
Municipal Year Book, 27

National Association of Pension Funds, 55
NHS concessions, 159
national insurance contributions, 91
– credited, 15, 38, 91, 101, 156, 157
– making, 73, 87, 91, 99, 140
– and pension, 56, 58
– qualifying number, 56, 91, 101, 102, 104, 150, 157
newspapers, reading, 25, 28
– adverts in, 28
notice
– of claiming redundancy, 81, 136
– giving, 7, 8
– leaving during, 119, 133, 134
– pay in lieu, 7, 83, 117, 119, 134, 139, 140, 141, 152, 163
– period required, 7, 67, 76, 117
– on redundancy, 134, 140 *et seq*, 163
– statutory, 7, 82, 117, 124, 134, 139

occupational pension *see* pension
Occupational Pensions Board, 56
Officers' Association, 22
Opportunities, 27
overtime, 52
– payment for, 63, 68, 83, 88, 161
– working, 77, 83, 92, 161

patents, 77
pay
– arrears of, 84, 86, 139
– awarded by tribunal, 119
– calculation of, 83
– deductions from, 69, 71, 86 *et seq*, 111
– entitlement to, 75, 80, 81, 84, 117, 134, 162
– equal, 77, 78, 84 *et seq*
– and hours worked, 78 *et seq*
– itemised statement of, 86, 87
– in lieu of notice, 7, 83, 117, 119, 134, 138, 139, 141, 152, 163
– low, 84
– maternity, 99
– medical suspension, 106
– method of getting, 87, 162
– and time off, 78, 79, 80, 108, 136
– timing of, 76, 162
– withheld, 84, 109, 111, 113
see also salary
PAYE, 87, 88, 145, 146
pension, 54 *et seq*, 76
– on changing jobs, 8, 9, 52, 54 *et seq*, 67, 68, 162
– contributions to, 55, 56, 57, 86, 103, 127, 162

– deferred, 9, 58 *et seq*, 66, 144
– information on, 52, 54, 55, 56, 59, 62, 63, 66
– money purchase scheme, 57, 58
– occupational, 55 *et seq*, 62, 63, 96, 140, 142, 152
– private plan, 61, 62
– on redundancy, 144
– refund, 58
– rights on dismissal, 123
– state, 55, 56, 57, 58, 62, 63, 91
– transferring, 55, 60 *et seq*, 66, 68
PER, 15, 18, 21, 23, 28
– courses, 16, 21
period of notice, 7, 67, 76, 82, 117, 124, 134, 139
perks, 69, 163
see also fringe benefits
personnel manager
– applying to, 26, 27
– giving information, 54, 68
– help from, 18, 141, 142
– and interviews, 41
– sifting applications, 18, 31, 32
Personnnel Management Yearbook, 24
piece worker, 83
police, job in, 28, 39, 74
polytechnic courses, 37
pregnancy, 91, 98 *et seq*, 119
– absence for, 82, 116
– and discrimination, 96
– returning to work after, 100, 101, 118
see also maternity
premiums
– life insurance, 40
– for medical insurance, 69, 90
– for pension plan, 62
prescribed industrial diseases, 104
preserved pension, 58, 66
private pension plan, 61, 62
probationary period, 67, 133
professional, 15, 21
– organisations, 16, 43, 69
– qualifications, 16, 30, 43, 70
– register of jobs, 22
protective award, 83, 127, 138, 139
public sector transfer club, 61

questions at interview, 47 *et seq*, 53
– preparing for, 42 *et seq*, 46

racial discrimination, 94 *et seq*
– and trade union, 92
rates, 147, 157
records, keeping, 33, 53
– of job applications, 13
– medical, 43
recruitment
– agencies, 11, 18, 19, 21
– consultants, 18, 23 *et seq*, 31, 33
– IPM code, 44, 45
red circling, 86
redundancy, 132 *et seq*
– effect of, 140, 141
– leaving early, 134, 141
– procedure, 68, 133 *et seq*
– selection for, 137, 138
– under notice of, 140 *et seq*
– volunteering for, 143, 144
redundancy payment, 73, 75, 133, 152, 157, 163
– calculating, 83, 132
– claiming, 81, 82, 127, 136 *et seq*, 139
re-engagement, 120, 131
referees, 33
– being approached, 44, 49, 52
– choosing, 19, 20
– employer as, 98, 143
– giving names of, 17, 20, 31
refund
– of pension, 58
– of tax, 88, 145, 146, 158
registering for employment, 15, 148
Regular Forces Employment Association, 22
reinstatement, 120, 130, 131
remedies *see* compensation, industrial tribunal
rent, 147, 157
replying to adverts, 29 *et seq*
resignation, 7, 8, 118, 134
restraint of trade, 77, 112, 163
retirement, 96
– death after, 64, 65
– and pension, 56 *et seq*, 71, 91, 103
– state age for, 56 *et seq*, 120, 121, 135

safety at work, 73, 99, 106 *et seq*
– representatives, 80, 107, 108
salary
– increase, 7, 8, 52, 67, 68
– negotiating, 51, 52, 54
– and new job, 35, 36, 67, 68, 162
– and pension, 8, 57, 59, 60, 62, 63, 64
– statement of, 86, 87
– and tax, 69, 88, 89
see also fringe benefits, pay
Scotland
– courts in, 112, 117, 124
– feu duty, 157
– industrial tribunals in, 128, 130
secretarial services, 70, 142, 161
self-assessment, 10 *et seq*
– and counselling, 11, 12
self-marketing, 12, 16, 29, 48, 53
see also c.v., letters of application
services, armed
– associations for, 22
– joining, 28, 39, 40
severance pay, 134
sex discrimination, 85, 86
– and union membership, 92
short-time, 81
sickness, 76, 82, 161
– benefit, 69, 91, 101, 102, 103, 152
– pay during, 101, 102, 103
see also, illness, injury
signing off, 159
signing on, 151, 153, 154, 157
social security offices, 101, 102, 105, 150, 158
Society of Pension Consultants, 62
solicitor, 113
– and industrial tribunal, 125, 131
– looking at contract, 37, 77
spent convictions, 98, 119
spouse, 13, 19, 143
– dependent, 150, 151, 153, 154
– as employer, 135
– and pension, 66, 150, 161
see also dependant
staff
– associations, 69, 70, 87, 93
– handbook, 7, 41, 55, 67, 70, 76
state pension, 55, 56, 57, 58, 62, 63
state help, 15 *et seq*
see also jobcentres, ESD, PER, MSC, supplementary benefit, TOPS, unemployment benefit
strikes, 80, 83, 92, 109, 110
– dismissal during, 110, 119, 135
– payment during, 110
Stock Exchange Yearbook, 26
supplementary benefit, 147, 157 *et seq*
– and exceptional need payment, 159
– when on strike, 109
Supplementary Benefits Handbook, 158
suspension
– as discipline, 111, 112, 113
– on medical grounds, 83, 106, 116, 127, 139

tax
– allowances, 87, 145
– coding, 87, 88, 145
– on compensation payments, 145
– deducted from pay, 87 *et seq*, 99
– on guarantee payment, 81
– limit on pensions, 62, 71
– office, 145, 146
– on pay in lieu of notice, 117, 145
– and pension contributions, 71
– and pension refund, 58
– on perks, 69, 88 *et seq*, 163
– planning advice, 144, 146 *et seq*
– on redundancy payment, 133, 145
– refund, 88, 145, 146, 158
– on state benefits, 102, 151
see also Inland Revenue, PAYE
telephone calls, 33, 35, 41, 46, 70
terms of contract, 67, 74 *et seq*, 117, 118
– and equality, 84, 85, 95
tests
– at interview, 49, 50
– vocational, 11
time limits for industrial tribunal claims, 126, 127
time off, 68, 73
– for antenatal care, 98, 99, 127
– to look for job, 127, 136, 139, 141, 144
– for maternity, 100, 127
– for public duties, 78, 79, 127
– for safety representatives, 108

– for training, 127, 136
– for union activities, 79, 80, 127, 139
Times Thousand, 26
TOE courses, 15
TOPS courses, 15, 37, 38
trade union
– and accidents at work, 105
– and closed shops, 93, 94
– collective bargaining, 74, 76, 79, 86, 101, 107, 138
– and discrimination, 92, 96
– and dismissal, 92, 93, 113, 119, 120, 131, 135
– expulsion/exclusion from, 93, 127, 131
– independent, 93, 107, 119
– membership of, 69, 87, 92 *et seq*, 119, 131
– and redundancies, 138
– representing, 110, 125, 156
– and trade disputes, 109, 110
– and unemployed members, 15, 22
training
– in job, 28, 52, 70, 89, 95, 163
– past, 10, 16, 30
– state, 15, 16, 37, 38
– while unemployed, 13, 14, 37, 142, 154
transferred pension, 55, 60 *et seq*, 66, 68
travelling to work, 35, 67, 68, 69, 83, 89, 90, 104, 133, 153, 159, 161, 163
Truck Acts, 84, 111
TSD, 15, 38
– leaflets, 38
TUC, 93
– handbook on Employment Act, 94
– and pensions, 55
– unemployed workers' centres, 15

unemployability supplement, 105
unemployed, being, 149 *et seq*
– routine while, 12 *et seq*, 33 *et seq*, 146, 147
unemployment benefit, 150 *et seq*
– claiming, 15, 149 *et seq*
– and compensatory award, 123, 130, 152
– disqualification from, 152, 154, 155, 156, 158
– forms for, 150, 151, 152, 153, 154, 156, 157, 159
– getting, 151, 152, 153, 156
– office, 134, 145, 149 *et seq*
– and redundancy payment, 133, 152
– stopping, 156, 157, 159
– and taking job, 153, 154
– when laid off, 81
– when not eligible for, 81, 91, 109, 117, 150, 151, 152
unfair dismissal *see* dismissal

vacancy, job, 25
– advertisements of, 16, 21, 22, 28 *et seq*
– at agencies, 20, 21, 22, 28, 35
vocational guidance, 11
voluntary
– pension contributions, 68, 71
– redundancy, 143, 144
– resignation, 7, 152
– work, 70, 153

waiting days, 152
wages *see* pay, salary
wages councils, 74, 84, 86
week, working, 68, 78
welfare of employees, 107
Which? reports
– on changing job, 9
– on employment law, 135
– on permanent health insurance, 103
– on personal pension plans, 62
– *Tax-Saving Guide*, 90
– on vocational guidance, 11
Who Owns Whom, 26
widow's pension, 57, 64, 65, 91, 102, 152, 161
witnesses, at industrial tribunal, 129, 130
women working, 78, 85, 86, 96
– and national insurance, 56, 91
see also discrimination, maternity
workless days, 80, 81
work-to-rule, 77, 109
written statement, 75 *et seq*, 110, 127
– of reason for dismissal, 119, 127
wrongful dismissal, 112, 117, 124

Earning money at home

for anyone who wants or needs to take up an activity at home that will bring some extra (or essential) cash, this book sets out what is entailed. It puts forward the pros and cons of working at home, stressing the self-discipline required and the reorganisation that may be necessary. The statutory requirements about planning permission, liability for insurance, national insurance and tax are all explained. Advertising and getting work, costing and charging for it, getting supplies, keeping accounts, are all important factors that are fully covered. The second section of the book suggests some types of work that might be suitable, with or without previous experience, giving a brief account of what may be involved in undertaking them. Courses for brushing up a skill or hobby to a more professional standard are suggested, and sources of further help and advice are given. The final section discusses what to do if your venture fares badly and, more optimistically, how to expand the business when successful.

Which? way to buy, sell and move house

takes you through all the stages of moving to another home—considering the pros and cons of different places, house hunting, viewing, having a survey, making an offer, getting a mortgage, completing the purchase, selling the present home. It explains the legal procedures and the likely costs. Buying and selling at an auction and in Scotland are specifically dealt with. The practical arrangements for the move and for any repairs or improvements to the new house are described. Advice is given for easing the tasks of sorting, packing and moving possessions, people and pets, with a removal firm or by doing it yourself, and for making the day of the move go smoothly.

The legal side of buying a house

for buying an owner-occupied house in England or Wales, this book will guide you step by step through the legal procedure. It explains what is involved and follows in detail the whole process of doing your own conveyancing. Even if you have decided that doing your own conveyancing would be too time-consuming or difficult for you, this book will help you check what your solicitor is doing at each stage. The book also deals with the legally less complicated procedure of selling your house.

Extending your house
describes what is involved in having an extension built on to a house or bungalow, and what has to be done, when and by whom. It explains how the Building Regulations affect the position and design of an extension, and how to apply to the local authority for planning permission and Building Regulations approval. For the technically-minded, various aspects of construction work are described, with a glossary and many explanatory drawings.

The Which? book of money
is a comprehensive layman's guide to money, giving practical expert advice on family finance of everyday concern, such as earnings, tax, life insurance, rates, borrowing, pensions, investments, grants, redundancy, passing money on.

Raising the money to buy your home
explains the choice of mortgage and lender that faces you when needing a loan to buy your first or a new home. It deals with building societies, banks, local authorities, insurance companies, warning about the limitations and conditions that each may impose. The book describes how interest rates can vary and shows, with tables, the difference between the quoted interest rate and what you actually pay. There are also calculations to enable you to work out your own payments on a repayment mortgage. The book takes you through the steps of applying for a loan, and deals with what happens if you have difficulty with keeping up the payments or want to pay off your mortgage.

Cutting your cost of living
suggests ways of spending less money without changing your standard of living. The book includes ideas on how to reduce your bills for food, toiletries, heating and holidays. There is a section on managing your money, and practical advice is given on growing your own fruit and vegetables, and on what jobs it is worth doing yourself.

On getting divorced
explains the procedure for getting a divorce in England or Wales, and how, in a straightforward undefended case, it can be done by the postal procedure. The legal advice scheme and other state help for someone with a low income is described and there is advice on coping in reduced circumstances. Calculations for maintenance and division of property

are given, with details of the orders the court may make for financial settlements between the divorcing couple and for arrangements about the children.

Avoiding heart trouble
identifies the factors which make a person more likely to develop heart trouble and describes how the various risk factors interact: cigarette smoking, raised blood pressure, high level of blood fats, stress, hereditary and dietary factors, oral contraceptives, overweight. It warns of the more serious signs and symptoms of heart trouble and, where possible, tells you what can be done about them.

Living through middle age
faces up to the physical changes and psychological difficulties for both men and women that this stage of life may bring (some inevitable, and some avoidable). Throughout, practical advice is given on overcoming problems, so that you can make the most of your middle years.

Avoiding back trouble
tells you about the spine and what can go wrong with the lower back. It deals with causes of back trouble, and gives hints on general care of the back when sitting, standing, lifting, carrying, doing housework and gardening. It describes how to cope with an attack of acute back pain, and discusses specialist examination and treatment, giving advice on how to avoid becoming a chronic sufferer and on exercises to strengthen and mobilise your spine.

Which? way to slim
is the complete guide to losing weight and staying slim. The book gives a balanced view of essentials such as suitable weight ranges, target weights, exercise, and the advantages and disadvantages of the different methods of dieting. The book highlights the dangers of being overweight and warns of the risks in middle age, during pregnancy, when giving up smoking.

What to do when someone dies
explains about doctors' certificates, about deaths reported to the coroner and what this entails, about registering a death and getting the various certificates that may be needed afterwards. Differences between burial and cremation procedure are discussed, and the

arrangements that have to be made, mainly through the undertaker, for the funeral. The book details the various national insurance benefits that may be claimed.

Wills and probate
is a book about wills and how to make them and about the administration of an estate by executors without the help of a solicitor. It explains clearly about interpreting the will, the valuation of the estate, payment of estate duty, what is involved in obtaining probate, and the distribution of the estate. It also shows, with examples, how to prepare a will, sign it, and have it witnessed. The final section deals with intestacy.

Other titles include

Central heating
Where to live after retirement
Pregnancy month by month
The newborn baby

All these publications are available from
Consumers' Association, Caxton Hill, Hertford SG13 7LZ
and from booksellers.